AUTHORS UNCOVERED

AUTHORS UNCOVERED

Popular Children's Authors from the USA & Canada

David J. Hallam-Jones

© David J. Hallam-Jones, 2022

Published by Vicuña Books UK

A CIP catalogue record for this book is available from the British Library.

ISBN 978-1-7399125-1-2

Book layout and cover design by Clare Brayshaw

Cover images © Vasilyrosca, © Blotty | Dreamstime.com

Prepared and printed by:

York Publishing Services Ltd
64 Hallfield Road
Layerthorpe
York YO31 7ZQ

Tel: 01904 431213

Website: www.yps-publishing.co.uk

Also available – Authors Uncovered: Britain's Favourite Children's Authors, Jack E. Heywood Vicuña Books UK (2021) ISBN 978-1-7399125-0-5

Contents

The authors are listed in order of their date of birth i.e. the most recently born individual is shown last.

Foreword

I can almost guarantee that you'll enjoy this second "Authors Uncovered" book as much as you did the first one.

Why? Firstly, because you're likely to get a better understanding of the world that these authors lived in (or still live in). Secondly, because you are likely to end up with a greater appreciation of how they and some of their characters tackled difficulties that they faced and then thirdly, by reading about the lives of the writers who have written humorous books you'll be reminded of the fun and craziness that life can offer.

Also, the more that we read and write, the better we are likely to become at expressing ourselves, something that is going to be really important for us in the future. After all, we are the world's future citizens.

I belong to the S.O.S. from the Kids choir – www.sosfromthekids.com – that aims to show individuals how much danger our planet is in so that they will want to do as much as they can to protect it. So I hope that reading this book will encourage you to become more confident in expressing yourself and in speaking up for things that you believe are important, including helping our precious planet.

Thank you for taking the time to have a look at the S.O.S. from the Kids website (if you do) and for encouraging your friends to do so too because our planet needs your help.

Sim Macaulay

Introduction

As a result of realising that most 8-12 year olds didn't know very much about the lives of a great number of children's authors my 10 year old grandson decided to turn his research on various British writers into book form. Thus "Authors Uncovered: Britain's Favourite Children's Authors" by Jack E. Heywood was born out of a 'home school' project completed during the Covid related school closures of 2020-2021.

Later, when I realised how many British authors had been inspired by some of the books written by American and Canadian authors, I decided to explore the backgrounds of some of these North American writers for the benefit of 8-13 year olds. What I discovered fascinated me and it led me to write the book that you are now holding. I have learned a lot from writing it and I hope that you will enjoy it and learn a lot from it.

Finally, if it helps you to realise that you could write a book of your own that would be great. After all your voices are going to need to be heard in the future and so I hope that as a result of even more reading and writing you will get even better at expressing yourself.

David J. Hallam-Jones
Nottingham, England.

Acknowledgements

I am particularly grateful to the following individuals for verifying the content of the relevant profiles: Robert Munsch, Kathleen Pearson (a.k.a. Kit Pearson), Daniel Handler (a.k.a. Lemony Snicket), Jeff Kinney and Huck Scarry.

In addition, I would also like to thank Andrea Perrin, of Bob Munsch Enterprises Ltd. and Anna Cesary and Charles Kochman of Wimpy Kid Inc. for their help.

Herman Melville

(Born Herman Melvill)

- **Life span:** 1 August 1819 – 28 September 1891
- **Place of birth:** New York City, U.S.A.
- **First book:** Typee (1846)

Although Herman's parents were born in the U.S. his father, Allan, who was an importer of luxury goods and fabrics from Europe had a Scots background. His mother the family homemaker (1), whose name at birth had been Maria Gansevoort, had a Dutch background. Allan and Maria had 8 children of which Herman was the third. After her husband's death and for some unknown reason Mrs Mevill decided to add a letter e to the end of their surname.

Herman had an older brother, Gansevoort, born in 1815, an older sister Helen born in 1817 and five younger siblings.

Herman's early life in Manhattan, New York seems to have been straightforward although when he was 7 years old he suffered from Scarlet Fever which permanently damaged his eyesight.

Herman spent some time attending New York Boys' High School with his older brother. Later on however, because his family were experiencing money problems they moved to Albany, New York State 240 kms (150 miles) away and the children changed schools. In an attempt to overcome their money problems his father became a partner in a fur hat company that included a factory and a fur hat shop. In addition to normal subjects Herman also studied Greek, Roman history and Jewish antiquities at Albany Academy and it was whilst he was at this school, aged 11 or 12 years old, that he developed an interest in writing.

However, his father died when Herman was 13 and his 16 yr old brother was compelled to take over running the family business. Their mother continued to look after the children and Herman left school to work in a bank to earn a wage. Luck though was not on their side and soon afterwards a fire destroyed the factory and his older brother had to ask to him leave the bank to help to run the hat shop.

Even more bad luck followed and when Herman was 18 years old the family business collapsed and he found himself penniless. Although he had no experience of farming Herman took a job managing a farm for a short time until he obtained a teaching job at a secondary school 65 kms (40 miles) away from Albany. However, because he didn't enjoy teaching he left the school after a few months and returned home.

When he was 19 years old Herman decided to study for a basic surveying & engineering exam in the hopes of getting a job on a canal extension project and even though the family moved nearer to Lansingburgh Academy 13 kms (15 miles) away to make studying easier for him he wasn't successful in getting one of the jobs after all.

Instead, in May 1839, he signed up as a ship's boy on a cargo ship that was about to make a journey to Liverpool, England and back. This became the first of his many sea voyages, journeys that he would write about years later.

Once he arrived home he accepted a teaching job at an academy in East Greenbush 30kms (50 miles) from New York but because the school failed to pay him he gave the job up and went home in spring 1840.

Then when summer arrived Herman and a friend went to Galena, Illinois 100 kms (160 miles) east of Chicago to look for work but when they didn't find any they returned home before the winter. Although he did eventually find some casual work once it dawned on Herman that could simultaneously earn a regular wage, enjoy some adventures and gather material for the books that he planned to write he signed up to work on a whaling ship that was about to sail the Atlantic and Pacific oceans.

Although this was a huge adventure involving a journey across the south Atlantic, around Cape Horn, into the southern Pacific and northwards along the Chilean coast to the Galapagos Islands it was also very hard work. Catching a single 40-60 ton whale, cutting it up and boiling it to extract its oil took about three days. Whenever the ship was fully loaded it would sail into a port and transfer its barrels of oil into cargo ships which would take them back to the U.S.

In June 1842 when the ship dropped anchor off Nuku Hiva, one of the Marquesas Islands in the mid Pacific, Melville and a friend jumped ship (2) and journeyed into the interior of the island where they were held captive by some tribespeople for several weeks.

They eventually managed to escape and having been accepted on another ship that needed crew members they sailed to Tahiti 1,500 kms (900 miles) away. However, by the time they arrived the crew were completely fed up and they mutinied (3) which resulted in Melville being jailed. After his release however, he and his friend spent a month as beach bums (4) on a neighbouring island.

In November 1842, when he had had spent enough time resting, Melville signed up for a further 5 month whaling voyage in the Pacific before leaving the ship in Hawaii. Then, perhaps feeling homesick after more than two years of casual work and several months in Honolulu, he enlisted as a sailor on the U.S. Navy ship that was heading back to the U.S.A. Discipline on board this ship was much more severe however, and he was forced to watch 163 disciplinary floggings that took place on board during the long 14 month journey home.

In October 1844, aged 25, he settled down at home to write about his adventures and during the next 12 years he wrote nine novels about his voyages, including his most famous book Moby Dick (1851).

This book was inspired by real-life events that he had read about concerning an albino sperm whale (5) named Mocha Dick that attacked whaling ships in the Pacific Ocean. Although the book was published in two countries in 1851 – as "The Whale" in England and as "Moby-Dick" in the U.S.A. – it was not very popular and it was only after his death that more people began to appreciate it.

During this period he and his fiancee Elizabeth Knapp Shaw married and in 1847 they bought a house in New York in which they raised their four children.

He continued writing until the end of his life, although when publishers found that they were no longer making large enough profits from his novels they became less interested in publishing his books and many of his later stories and poems appeared in magazines instead.

Between 1857-59 and as a means of earning money he began to give public lectures about his sea adventures and his recent visits to Istanbul, Egypt, Palestine, Jordan and parts of Europe. Next though, because he was still not earning enough money to support his family he accepted a job as a Customs Officer (6) in New York, a job that he kept for nearly 20 years.

Although he worked hard at his job worry, tiredness and pain, plus drinking too much alcohol, often left Melville short-tempered and sometimes he mistreated his family and servants.

Billy Budd, Melville's last short novel lay unfinished in a box for more than 25 years after his death and a revised version of it only became available in 1962 as the result of the efforts of various scholars to sort out its muddled state. Since then some people have described it as Melville's next best book after Moby Dick.

Popular versions of Moby Dick and Billy Budd have been adapted for the stage, for opera houses, for cinema screens and on television.

Although he didn't earn either fame or fortune during his lifetime the public became more interested in his work after his death and today he is regarded as one of America's greatest writers.

Whereas he died of a heart problem in New York at the age of 72 his wife lived for a further 15 years.

"A book in one's brain is better than a book bound in a calf-skin (leather) cover."
Herman Melville

Louisa May Alcott

- **Life span:** 29 November 1832 – 6 March 1888
- **Born:** Germantown, Philadelphia, U.S.A.
- **First book:** Moods (1864)

When she was born Louisa's father Amos Alcott was a part-time teacher and a philosopher (7). Her mother Abigail was a part-time welfare assistant working with Irish immigrants. She once described her husband as "like a man in a hot air balloon who could generally be relied upon as long as there were three women on the ground holding the ropes." They had four daughters of which Louisa was the second oldest.

The family was quite poor and they moved 22 times in 30 years living in different cities whilst their parents looked for jobs and better lives. When Louisa was 2 yrs old the family moved to Boston where Mr Alcott tried to establish a school. However, this wasn't a success and neither was the 7 month long Fruitlands Commune project (8) that he and some friends attempted to establish near Harvard, Massachusetts in 1843.

Although the Alcott girls were educated by their parents they were also exposed to some new and different ways of thinking about the world by some of the most influential thinkers of that era through a number of their father's friends and as a result they learned to question many of the traditional views and rules for living put forward by leaders of that time.

As a result of these influences the girls grew up to reject slavery and the drinking of alcohol. Neither did they accept the idea that women were inferior to men or that women were not allowed to vote.

Not that Louisa needed any encouragement to think and behave differently to other children. As a child and as a teenager her parents found her more boisterous than her sisters and she frequently challenged the existing rules about how women should behave. For example, as an adult writer she even encouraged her female readers to run, something that was not considered lady-like.

Because the family was poor the sisters had to find small jobs to earn money and Louise accepted needlework, child care, domestic work and teaching to help. This was also when she started creative writing to help her deal with her unhappiness and her frustration about life.

By the time she was 15 years old not only was she was a part-time teacher but she and her family were also involved in helping runaway slaves to escape to other parts of America to gain their freedom.

As a teenager Louisa wrote a collection of stories entitled Flower Fables but these were not published until later. However, by the time she was 28 years old some of her stories and poems had begun to appear in the Atlantic Monthly magazine.

When the Civil War (1861-65) began, a war fought between the northern states and the southern states mainly over slavery, Louisa moved to Washington D.C. to serve as as a volunteer nurse. However, she had to leave after six weeks because she caught typhoid fever. The disease and the treatment left her unwell for much of the rest her life and even though she still wasn't completely well in 1865 she accepted a job as a travelling companion and spent a year touring Europe with an invalid lady.

The period 1863-86 was when Alcott wrote most of the books for which she became famous. In 1863 she wrote about her experiences as a nurse in a Boston newspaper and this was followed by her first book.

Early on during her career she wrote more than thirty thrillers for adult readers using the pen name A. M. Barnard and in 1865 she created one of the earliest detective fiction stories written in America entitled "V.V., or Plots and Counterplots". However, in 1865 in an entry in her diary she also described some of her writing as "well paid rubbish".

After her return from Europe at the age of 35 years old she became the editor and a contributor to an illustrated children's magazine called Merry's Museum. This was when she returned to writing mostly for children.

It was not though until 1868 that her publisher asked her to write "a girls' story". Surprisingly, having agreed to do this she wrote the first part of Little Women (1868) in 10 weeks. The book was based on her experiences of growing up with her three sisters and it was so successful that readers soon demanded another part. As a result she wrote a sequel about the lives of four fictitious sisters that was published as Good Wives (1869).

Once rich she and her younger sister were able to make a second visit to Europe and she wrote Little Men (1871) whilst they were staying in Rome. Her third book was about Jo's experience of starting a school with her husband and her final book in the March family series was called Jo's boys (1886).

Her readers loved the free and positive spirit that she wrote about in her books that reflected her love of nature, freedom and life.

However, in addition to her writing she never gave up fighting for equal rights for everyone or the right for women to vote. In fact in 1877 she was one of the founders of the Women's Educational and Industrial Union (9) in Boston.

Although Alcott never married or had any children when she was 43 years old she adopted her 8 year old niece after her sister May died of a fever and she cared for "Lulu" for eight years.

Louisa died at home at the age of 55 years old as the result of a stroke (10) two days after her father's death.

The popularity and success that Alcott achieved for Little Women is reflected in the fact that 2,347 editions of her book have been produced between 1800-2020 in 25 languages. In addition, five films, five stage plays, four television series, two cartoon versions, a BBC Radio version, several audiobook versions and several documentaries concerning this particular book have been produced. Little Men inspired three film versions and a television series and therefore very few people were surprised when her name was included in the National Women's Hall of Fame in 1996.

"Women who dare are few, whilst women who stand and wait are many."
L.M. Alcot

Samuel Langhorne Clemens

(a.k.a. Mark Twain)

- **Life span:** 30 November 1835 – 21 April 1910
- **Born:** Florida, Missouri, U.S.A.
- **First book:** The Innocents Abroad (1869)

Mark, as he became known later, was the sixth of seven children whose parents Jane and John Clemens were married in 1832. Sadly however, four of the family died prematurely including three of his siblings and their father. His father had become a lawyer at the age of 21 years and a county judge prior to his death at the age of 49.

When he was 4 years old 'Mark' and his family moved to Hannibal, a town at the side of the Mississippi River which he renamed St. Petersburg in his children's books. It was here that he fell in love with the excitement of river life, something that would draw him back to it later like a magnet.

The early and unexpected death of his father in 1847 left the family with almost no money to live on and because of this Mark had to leave school and begin work at the age of 11 or 12.

To help improve the family's finances his oldest brother bought a newspaper company and Mark became an apprentice printer for him and later a typesetter (11). This was how he began his writing career because he also submitted short pieces and humorous stories to their newspaper.

However, when he was 18 yrs he decided to leave Hannibal to see more of this vast country and to improve his skills. So he spent the next couple of years in various U.S. cities working as a casually employed typesetter whilst improving his education by using public libraries in the evenings.

By the time he was 22 years old his dream of working on one of the large steam boats that plied their way up and down sections of the Mississippi River overwhelmed him and he moved to St Louis for two years to train as a river pilot. Although he had to pay an experienced pilot to train him he gained his licence in 1858. It was also at this time that he started to use this unusual pen-name Mark Twain (12).

He loved working on the world's second longest river 1,930 kms (1,200 miles), something that he wrote about later in 'Life on the Mississippi' (1883) and he continued working on steamboats between St Louis and New Orleans until the Civil War began in 1861 when military activity on the river restricted the movement of shipping.

At the outbreak of the war Twain decided to go to Nevada to join his oldest brother who had become an important government official there. However having failed in an attempt to become a miner he began writing for newspapers again producing amusing pieces that led him to become well-known. Not only did he earn praise from other writers and his critics but he was also befriended by presidents, industrialists and European royalty, all of whom who enjoyed his writing.

Many people refer to him as "the Father of American literature" because his use of satire (13) encouraged other authors see that it was acceptable to use different writing styles, something that gave them more freedom in their writing.

His creative writing, his speeches and his lectures were so highly thought of that he made a lot of money quite easily. However, because he was not very good at looking after his money he also lost lots of it through unsuccessful projects.

Due to the popularity of his writing he was invited to visit Hawaii in 1865. This was followed by a five and a half month speaking tour in 1867 during which time he visited London, parts of Europe and The Holy Land.

Whilst he was on tour in 1867 he saw a photograph of Olivia Langdon, a wealthy businessman's daughter from New York State. She was the sister of a friend of his and as a result of seeing her picture he fell passionately in love with her and became determined to marry her. Their marriage took place in 1870.

For their first date records show that Twain took Olivia to listen to Charles Dickens the famous English author giving a public reading of some of his work at a venue in New York City.

The couple had three daughters and a son although sadly their son died of diphtheria at the age of 19 months old and two of their daughters died in their 20s.

Between 1874-91 he and his family lived in a house in Hartford, Connecticut that had been specially designed for them and this was where he wrote many of his best-known books, including The Adventures of Tom Sawyer (1875) and The Adventures of Huckleberry Finn (1885).

However, although 74 editions of The Adventures of Tom Sawyer were published in three languages between 1875 -1997 he was always short of money.

As a result of this between 1891- 99 he and his wife completed several world tours to parts of Europe and Canada; Fiji, Australia, New Zealand, Sri Lanka, India, Mauritius and South Africa so that Twain could give lectures and earn enough money to pay off their debts. Sadly though one of their daughters, Susy, died of meningitis in 1896 before the family could return to home to Hartford and as a result they chose never to live in this house again and instead spent the rest of their lives abroad.

Twain's wife died in 1904 and he died six years later aged 75 as the result of a heart attack. This was not however, before he was awarded an honorary degree by the University of Oxford in 1907. This followed him being awarded an honorary degree by Yale University in the USA in 1888.

Although some of Twain's writing and his views were sometimes criticised and his books were occasionally banned most people saw him as someone who held views that where not uncommon at that time rather than as someone who intended to deliberately offend others.

"Sail away from the safe harbour. Catch the trade winds in your sails. Explore. Dream. Discover."
S. L. Clemens (a.k.a. Mark Twain)

Lyman Frank Baum

(a.k.a. L. Frank Baum)

- **Life span:** 15 May 1856 – 6 May 1919
- **Born:** Chittenango, New York State, U.S.A.
- **First book:** The Book of the Hamburgs (1886)

Frank, as he preferred to be called, was his parents' seventh child. His father Benjamin was 35 years old when Frank was born and his mother, who was the family homemaker (1), was 36 yrs old. His parents had nine children in total although five of them died prematurely, something that frequently happened in that era.

His father made a fortune from oil drilling and oil sales and 1861, when Frank was 5 years old the family bought a large mansion in Mattydale, New York State. Whilst they were young he and his siblings were educated at home by private tutors. However, when he was 9 years old he was sent to Peekskill Military Academy, in Westchester County, a private school for boys on Oak Hill which overlooks the Hudson River. However, when he was 11 he was sent home because a longstanding heart problem meant that he couldn't cope with the school's programme of physical activities.

It seems that new pupils who had travelled up river by steamboat from New York to Peekskill Landing were often advised by local people to "follow the yellow brick road" in order to reach the school. Thus, the fact that the road was made of Dutch pavers, stone blocks with a yellowish hue, is said to have inspired Frank to use the phrase "Follow the yellow brick road" in his Oz stories.

In his spare time and after his father had bought him a cheap printing press for his 11th birthday he and his younger brother produced their own newspaper The Rose Lawn Home Journal. It carried advertisements from local businesses and they gave copies of it away free of charge between 1870-1873. Later on, at the age of 13 years, as the result of having developed an interest in collecting and selling used stamps he published a journal called The Stamp Collector. He followed this in 1873 by publishing a booklet called Baum's Complete Stamp Dealers' Directory.

Finally, and perhaps to round off his early publishing experiments, he created another journal The Poultry Record when he was 21 years old. A craze for breeding exotic poultry was sweeping the country at this time and Frank himself had began rearing Hamburg chickens.

He particularly enjoyed books and plays by Charles Dickens and he was soon experimenting with acting. His father owned a number of theatres and opera houses and as a result, once Benjamin had accepted that his son might become a successful actor and an impresario (14) he built a theatre for him and Frank put on a number of successful plays in it including one of his own.

However, his theatrical company eventually ran into financial difficulties he and his new wife moved to Aberdeen, South Dakota where some family members of his wife's lived and he opened a small hardware shop. This also failed after a short while and instead he published his own local newspaper until a wheat crop failure meant that most of his customers could no longer afford to buy newspapers.

Unfortunately he also suggested in his newspaper, on several occasions, that all American natives i.e. Indian tribes people should be exterminated to protect the white population who had taken over large parts of America, statements that his family later apologised for.

Next Frank, his wife and their four boys moved to Chicago. This was where the the World Fair was being held in 1893 and where Frank thought he would be able to find work. He became a reporter for a newspaper but once he realised that he was not earning a enough money to support his family he took a job as a travelling salesman for an ornamental glass manufacturer.

Whenever he was at home however, his children and various local children would badger him to tell them stories. Because of this his mother-in-law suggested to him that he should down write some of his stories and publish them, including those he wrote whilst he was away from home staying in hotels.

At this time Frank, whose health wasn't very good, consulted a heart specialist. The doctor advised him to give up his travelling salesman's job and to stop smoking cigars and so, following his mother-in-law's earlier advice he gave up his job and wrote his first story: Mother Goose in Prose (1897). He followed this up with a book of nonsense poems entitled Father Goose: His Book (1899) which was illustrated by Mr W.W. Denslow, a gifted illustrator. This second book was so successful that the two men continued working together for several years eventually creating their famous non-frightening fairytale: The Wonderful Wizard of Oz in 1900.

Frank produced seventeen Oz sequels but because he wanted to experiment with other types of fantasy fiction he would occasionally announce that his latest Oz book would be his last, only to write another one in the series before too long because the series was so popular and because his other books never sold as well. However, what he really wanted to do was to try writing stories in other styles without having to worry about whether they would be successful or profitable.

In fact he did write some 'non-Oz' books using various pen names including Aunt Jane's Nieces (1906-18), a series of ten books for young teenage girls under the name of Edith Van Dyne.

Despite his successful writing he never managed to keep much money in his bank account because he very rarely made any profit from his other entertainment ventures, including his theatre plays. It was these losses and setbacks that forced for him to keep writing his Oz stories.

In 1910 when Frank 54 and his wife was 49 they decided to move from Chicago to Los Angeles and after a short while they bought a plot of ground in a quiet village called Hollywood that was surrounded by citrus orchards. There they built a two-storey wooden house that they christened "Ozcot" and once they had settled into it Frank enjoyed a quieter life of gardening, golf and writing until 1914.

Later he started the Oz Film Manufacturing Company of Hollywood in an attempt to provide an alternative to the violent cowboy films commonly watched by American children. However, the company was not a success and Frank eventually passed it on to their eldest son Frank J. Baum.

By 1917 his health was worse and he was alternating between being in bed in hospital or being in bed at home. However, despite his heart problem and breathing difficulties he was still smoking cigars at the same time as taking strong painkillers. Finally, after finishing his last book Glinda of Oz in early May 1919 he died quietly at the age of 62 years. His wife however, continued living until she was 91 yrs old.

In total Baum wrote 13 novels in the Oz series plus 55 other novels (not including four others that were lost and went unpublished), 83 short stories, over 200 poems and at least 42 scripts. Many of his books, stories, poems and scripts were published using one of his seven pen names. Eight films have been made from his books including The Wizard of Oz (1939) which starred Judy Garland as Dorothy, a film has been referred to as one of the greatest films in cinema history.

In 1976 the Chicago city authorities named a new 13-acre park Oz Park in his honour and in 2013 Baum was given a memorial place in the Chicago Literary Hall of Fame. In addition his fame lives on through a Wizard of Oz themed festival that is held in Baum's birthplace each year during first weekend of June, something that no doubt would have pleased him.

*"I believe is that day dreams are likely to lead
to the betterment of the world."*
L. F. Baum

Laura Elizabeth Ingalls-Wilder

- **Life span:** 7 February 1867 – 10 February 1957
- **Birthplace:** Pepin, Wisconsin, U.S.A.
- **First book:** Little House in the Big Woods (1932)

Laura's father Charles Ingalls was a farmer and his wife Caroline was a teacher. They married when they were 24 years old and they had four daughters who survived childhood, of whom Laura was the second oldest. Their fifth child was a little boy who became ill and died when he was 9 months old, as many infants did at that time.

When Laura was 2 years old her father, who was always searching for opportunities to improve their lives, took the family across the centre of America from Wisconsin to Minnesota in a canvas hooded waggon pulled by mules. His plan was to create a new farm on a plot of previously uncultivated land in the Midwest. However, this project wasn't very successful and they returned to Wisconsin in 1871. Nevertheless these hard and exciting journeys across The Great Plains (15) made a huge impression on Laura who would write about these journeys and events much later.

In 1874 Laura's father decided to move the family to the small town called Walnut Grove in Minnesota consisting almost entirely of wooden buildings and for a short time the Ingalls lived in a dug-out home (16) on the edge of the town. They eventually built a log cabin in the same field but after their crops had failed for a second year Charles decided to move his family to Burr Oak, a small town in Iowa where he became the part owner of a hotel.

Their father's restlessness didn't subside until much later however, and their next move was back to Walnut Grove where they had lived three years earlier, i.e. in the log cabin next to their earthen dug-out.

They stayed there until Laura was 12 when her father decided to move them again, this time to the part of midwest America now called South Dakota. There, once he had found a spot that he liked on the edge of the vast empty prairie 30 minutes walk from the small town of De Smet, Mr Ingalls began to build a part-stone and part-log cabin that became their "little house on the prairie".

This was where they finally settled and where Laura was able to finish her schooling and make some permanent friends. Although only 15 years old at the time Laura also had to take on several part-time jobs to earn extra money for the family. These were the times that she wrote about in her two books Little Town on the Prairie (1941) and These Happy Golden Years (1943). It was also during this time that she met the man who eventually become her husband, Almanzo Wilder.

The Midwest suffered an extremely severe winter in 1881 and it was cut off by blizzards from December until the following May. This prevented trains from reaching the town, something that Laura would also wrote about later.

In 1842, whilst Laura was still only 15 years old she obtained a certificate and became the teacher in a single room country school 20 kms (12 miles) south of De Smet.

During this period her boyfriend Almanzo, who was 10 years older than her, often drove her to school on his waggon – or his sleigh in the winter – and he would also pick Laura up and drive her back to her parents' home for weekends. However, when they were married in 1885 Laura gave up her teaching job in De Smet to help her new husband on his farm.

Most settlers had to endure hardships and uncertainties on the vast wild plains of the midwest and the Wilders didn't escape their share of tragedies and misfortunes. For example in 1889 their new baby died 12 days after his birth. More misfortune followed later with Almanzo suffering partial paralysis in his legs after developing diphtheria (17). Finally their house accidentally burned down.

Because of this they lived with Almanzo's parents for almost a year although eventually they decided to move to Florida in 1891 to make a fresh start. However, the extremely dry climate prevented them from succeeding in growing any crops on their new farm and after a year they returned northwards, first to De Smet and finally to Missouri where they lived for the rest of their lives.

The farm house – Rocky Ridge Farm near Mansfield, Missouri – was an uninhabitable windowless log cabin when they bought it, but over the next 20 years they worked hard to remodel it into a 10-room house and to create a successful poultry, dairy and fruit farm.

Once the the farm was a functioning successfully not only did Laura use some of her spare time to help with with community projects but she also began writing again. At first she wrote about home-making, farming and country life for a local magazine for which she was also the home editor of between 1911-23.

In 1929 when millions of Americans including the Ingalls-Wilder family were struggling financially because of a huge stock market crash (18) Laura and her daughter Rose decided instead to work on improving the content of Laura's journals to see if they could make some money from selling copies of a book that they decide to call Pioneer Girl. An editor advised Laura to convert her writing into stories for children even if these were not always completely true. The two women gradually produced a series of stories for 8-12 year olds and although Laura wasn't always happy with the changes that she felt compelled to make, her books soon became popular and earned them a great deal of money.

In 1935 although Laura's daughter moved away from Rocky Ridge Farm to live elsewhere the the two women continued working on the "Little House stories" through writing letters to each other. The stories were completed in 1943 by which time Laura was 76 years old.

From then on the Ingalls-Wilders reduced the amount of work they did on the farm and carried on living independently without any financial worries. Almanzo died in 1949, aged 92 yrs, after which Laura continued to live alone on their farm for the next eight years.

In February 1957 Laura fell ill and had to spend a few days in hospital. Sadly though she died three days after her 90th birthday soon after her daughter had brought her home.

It is estimated that the books from the Little House series have sold over 60 million copies in more than 100 countries and have been translated into at least nine languages. Many programmes about Wilder and her books have also been produced for the stage and screen including a twelve part American television series: Little House on the Prairie (1974-84) and a 26 part cartoon series in Japanese: Laura, the Prairie Girl (1975-76).

In 1954, the American Library Association introduced an award for children's writers and illustrators, named after Wilder and she was the first person to receive it. The Laura Ingalls Wilder Medal recognises living authors or illustrators whose books, published in the United States, have made "a substantial and lasting contribution to literature for children". In 2018 however, the award was renamed the Children's Literature Legacy Award because it was felt that some of the language used in Laura's books didn't reflect the cruel ways in which many Native Americans and African Americans had been mistreated by white Americans over many years.

"No one has ever achieved anything from the smallest wish to their greatest unless their dream was dreamed first of all."

L. Ingalls-Wilder

Eleanor Emily Hodgman-Porter

(born Hodgman)

- **Life span:** 19 December 1868 – 21 May 1920
- **Born:** Littleton, New Hampshire, U.S.A.
- **First book:** Cross Currents (1907)

Between 1865 -70 Eleanor's father Francis ran two businesses in the village of Littleton, a combined jewellery & watchmaker's shop and a drug store (19). Her mother Llewella may have helped in the shops although the couple also had an older son, Frederick, living at home.

Although Eleanor (a.k.a Nellie) was good at creative writing from a very early age her first love was music. She was a weak girl and her education was cut short when she became ill and had to her to leave her secondary school to some spend time recovering in the clean air of a mountainous area nearby. However, once she was a little better she was taught at home by private tutors. Later another tutor gave her singing lessons at home after which she studied at the New England Conservatory of Music in Boston. In fact, she became such good singer that she began to teach singing and also became well known locally for singing in private homes, church choirs and in public concerts

When she was 24 years old she married John Lyman Porter, the director of a machine manufacturing company. Then, because of his work commitments, they spent the next 10 years living in various cities in the eastern United States before moving into an apartment in Cambridge, Massachusetts which they shared with Eleanor's invalid mother.

In the early 1900s Eleanor decided to stop singing in public and teaching music because of her mother needed more help and she began writing short stories. By 1915 she had written more than 200 short stories including some using her pen-name Eleanor Stewart.

Although she published her first novel in 1907 her first big success was with Miss Billy (1911), the tale of a girl who changes the lives of three bachelor brothers with whom she went to live.

However, after the publication of several less-successful books it was the story of an endlessly optimistic orphan called Pollyanna that made Eleanor famous. These stories proved so popular when they were serialised in a weekly magazine that in 1920 she agreed for them to be published as a book. Over one million copies were sold very quickly and since then, i.e. between 1912 – 2020 572 editions of this one book have been published. It has also been translated into more than six languages and some editions have been reprinted many times.

The book's success led Hodgson-Porter to write Pollyanna Grows Up (1915) and this was followed by eleven more Pollyanna sequels known as "The Glad Books".

Next she wrote Just David (1916), a book about an orphan boy who used his extraordinary talent as a violinist to restore order to a particular community and to heal broken relationships. Through her book she hoped to help boys to understand the value of having an optimistic approach to everyday life. Her final books were Road to Understanding (1917); Oh, Money! Money! (1918); Dawn (1919); and Mary Marie (1920).

Her belief that an individual can change the world into a better place through sheer determination came from the "glad game" that she used to play with her father. When she had complained to her father once that she had only been able to find a pair of crutches in a charity box and not the doll she hoped to find her father told her that she should always try to always look on the bright side of situations and that in that instance she needed to be glad that she didn't need the crutches.

Although Hodgson-Porter also wrote a number of novels and short-story collections for adults she is best known for her Pollyanna stories, some versions of which continue to be printed and digitally formatted even today. Pollyanna has also been produced for theatres, cinemas and television.

Eleanor Hodgman Porter died of tuberculosis (20) at home in Cambridge, Massachusetts at the age of 51. She left no husband or children.

"The influence of a beautiful, helpful, hopeful character is contagious. People radiate what is in their minds and in their hearts."

E. Hodgman-Porter

Lucy Maud Montgomery

- **Life span:** 30 November 1874 – 24 April 1942
- **Birthplace:** Clifton, Prince Edward Island, Canada
- **First book:** Anne of Green Gables (1908)

Although Maud (her preferred name) had Canadian parents one of her grandmothers was an English woman who had moved to Canada from Suffolk, England as a child. This lady grew up and had six children one of whom was Maud's mother Clara. Clara died of tuberculosis (20) before Maud was 2 years old leaving her father to cope with the toddler. However, because of his work her father found it necessary to leave the little girl to be cared for by her English grandmother on this beautiful but bleak island whilst he continued to live and work nearby. However, when Maud was 7 years old Hugh Montgomery moved to another part of Canada 4,800 kms (3,000 miles) away and remarried leaving Maud in the care of her grandparents.

Fortunately her grandparents had two orphaned boys of Maud's age living with them and so between the ages of 7-11 Maud enjoyed four fun-filled years with the boys and various cousins until the grandparents decided it was time for the boys to live elsewhere.

Maud spent much more time alone once the boys had left and she created imaginary friends and fantasy worlds to help her to cope with her loneliness. When she was 12 years old Maud submitted a poem for publication to a local newspaper and although she was disappointed when it was rejected she nontheless felt that her writing would eventually be appreciated.

When she was 16 and had completed her schooling Maud was invited to spend a year with her father and Mary his 24 year old second wife in Canada's Central Lowlands, a six day train journey away. However, she neither enjoyed that year nor appreciated her new stepmother and as a result she was glad to return to live with her grandparents.

Maud loved the island and it was during some of her lonely walks that she began to experience the special closeness that she felt existed between nature and the heavenly powers. She also began to imagine Anne Shirley who would eventually become her famous fictional character.

During 1893-1894 she studied for a teaching qualification at a college on Prince Edward Island completing the two-year course in one year and graduating with honours.

Altogether she taught at three schools on the island although she stopped teaching for a year in 1895 to study several English literature courses at Dalhousie University in Halifax, Nova Scotia. In doing this she became one of the few women of that time to study at such a high level. The university was a five hour journey away and this adventure represented a huge change for a country girl.

Apparently she didn't really enjoy teaching in the one-room country schools although at least the lack of pressure allowed her plenty of spare time in which to develop her writing skills.

At the age of 23 years and perhaps because she was feeling anxious about being alone in the future she agreed to become engaged to be married to a distant cousin who was studying to be a Baptist Church minister (21). However, she soon regretted her decision and although she didn't break off their engagement she began a romance with another young man at the same time. Eventually she decided that it was wrong to have serious relationships with two young men at the same time and so she broke off her friendship with the second man.

In 1898 when her grandfather died Lucy returned to live with her grandmother to help her to run the post office that existed within her grandmother's home. She remained there for the next thirteen years with the exception of a nine-month period in 1901-1902 when she worked as a proof-reader (22) in a newspaper office in the city of Halifax.

During these 13 years not only was Maud able to help her grandma but she was also able to write 125 short stories and to publish the first of two books about the fictitious orphan Anne Shirley.

She submitted her draft of her first book to various publishers but following numerous rejections she decided to put it to one side. As a result it wasn't until 1908 that she found a publisher who would accept it which was when Anne of Green Gables was published. Fortunately it was an immediate success and over 19,000 copies of it were sold during its first five months. In addition, it had to be reprinted ten times before the end of 1909.

However, when her grandma died and her son inherited both the house and the post office business Maud had nowhere to live and no adult company. As a result she decided to accept an offer of marriage from a different church minister and she to move to Leaskdale in the state of Ontario after their honeymoon (23) in England and Scotland.

Although their house, which belonged to the church, was very basic and had no bathroom or toilet Maud raised two children in it whilst she was in her late 30s. She also wrote seven more books and fourteen short stories as a means of escaping her unhappiness. Her unhappiness was due to the fact that she and her husband were experiencing periods of poor mental health that were made worse by the stress of raising two young children at the same time as being responsible for all the church activities. In addition they were also affected by the First World War in Europe and the "Spanish Flu" pandemic.

Both World War I (1914-18) and the flu pandemic (1918-20) seriously affected Maud and when she wasn't ill she spent a lot of time writing articles and giving talks about the need for young Canadian men to go to France to fight against Germans. She also worked hard in the struggle to win the vote for women so that they would be able to influence the Canadian government's future plans.

1920-25 were difficult years for the family too because in addition to her career as a writer Maud was also trying to cope with her husband's mental health problems, helping him to run the church, dealing with their 10 year old and 13 year old sons and fighting a battle in the law courts against a dishonest publisher who had been cheating her out of her royalties (24). In 1925 a court agreed that she had been cheated and ordered the publisher to compensate her for her losses. However, in view of the stress that they were experiencing and the need to improve their lives Maud's husband agreed to move to a different church in Norval, near Toronto in 1926.

However, despite having a nicer home and more opportunities to enjoy shopping, theatres and social gatherings when Maud wasn't writing their family problems seemed worse. Her husband became too mentally ill to work and they had a lot of problems with their teenage son. Worst of all though was the fact that even though her books were selling well and several film studio owners were interested in turning her stories into films certain members of the Canadian Authors' Association criticised her publicly saying that she was only a children's writer and not than a proper novelist.

Soon after her husband's retirement in 1935 they moved to a different Toronto suburb and bought a new house that Maud named Journey's End. She was still only 61 years of age but perhaps she judged that this would be her last home?

At this time Canada seemed very likely would be drawn into World War II and Maud was extremely anxious about her sons being sent to fight in Europe. However, she continued to write and she published two further books in the Anne series in the mid-to-late 1930s and another an unrelated children's story, Jane of Lantern Hill (1939).

Outside of their home she put on a happy smiling face especially when talking to fans or lecturing to groups of people in different parts of Canada. However, when she was at home she could often be found in bed worrying. In fact that was where she was found following her death at the age of 68yrs.

In terms of sales during her lifetime and since her death Montgomery has remained the most successful Canadian author of all time having written 20 novels and over 500 short stories, i.e. with 14,584 publications in 25 languages during the period 1908-2020. However, even though her books made her a lot of money Maud always insisted that she had created these stories out of love and not to earn vast amounts of money.

Nonetheless she was enormously proud to have been instituted as the first female Canadian fellow of The Royal Society of Arts in 1923, to be awarded an O.B.E. in 1935, and to be designated a Person of National Historic Significance by the Canadian Government in 1943. In addition, the Lucy Maud Montgomery Primary School, Toronto and the Lucy Maud Montgomery Park, Toronto are named in her honour.

"Tomorrow is always fresh with no mistakes in it."
L.M. Montgomery

John Griffith Chaney

(a.k.a. Jack London)

- **Life span:** 12 January 1876 – 22 November 1916
- **Birth:** San Francisco, U.S.A.
- **First book:** The Son of the Wolf (1900)

Jack London, as he was known following his adoption as a baby, was initially cared for at a neighbour's house by an African-American neighbour who had previously been enslaved. This was because Jack's mother was not very well mentally at the time of her son's birth and the boy's father, an astrologer called William Chaney, denied that Jack was his son.

Later in 1876 Jack's mother married a retired soldier named John London who had two daughters of his own and Jack returned home to live as part of this new family.

Whilst he was attending West End Elementary School in the San Francisco suburb of Alameda he also received a lot of help from the staff at Oakland's public library who helped him to widen his reading. Then from 11-14 he attended Cole Grammar School in West Oakland.

He learnt to sail as the result of his stepfather taking him out in San Francisco bay and even before he was a teenager Jack had saved and borrowed a total of $300 for a small sailing dinghy.

When he was 15 years old his stepfather had a work accident and Jack was forced to leave school to earn a wage. He worked 14-16 hour days in a canning factory but he soon realised that he could escape factory work, enjoy sailing and make more money by becoming an oyster bed pirate. This involved stealing oysters from other fishermen's nets at night. However, he was eventually caught by the crew of a patrol boat and he agreed to accept a job with them.

At the age of 17 he signed up as a crew member on a sailing ship for a seven-month seal hunting trip off the coast of Japan and although he proved himself to be one of the best sailors onboard he decided not sign up for another voyage. He did however, submit a short story about his adventures in a local literacy competition and he won first prize, something that marked the beginning of his writing career.

Having returned to Oakland he worked in a jute mill (25) and later in a boiler room until he decided to join a large group of unemployed workers on a protest march to the U.S. capital Washington D.C. However, after deciding to leave the march early he became a tramp and he even went to jail for a month in New York State as a punishment for vagrancy (26).

But the degradation (27) that Jack witnessed in prison shocked him into realising that the only way to avoid remaining a vagrant was to fight his way out of poverty. So when he was released from jail at the age of 18 he returned to San Francisco determined to improve his education and despite having left school at 14 he began attending Oakland High School.

Despite the fact that the other children there viewed him as a shabby, tobacco-chewing vagrant he was determined to become a writer and as a result of a some time at the High School and three months of intensive revision in a cramming school (28) he was accepted by the University of California as a special student at the age of 19. However, he left after a year because he felt that he was resented by wealthier and better educated students who were jealous of his progress but also because his family needed him to earn money.

However, when he was not working long hours for poor wages he was soon writing and submitting short stories despite getting lots of rejections from publishers.

He worked hard to escape poverty helped by his belief in socialism (29) which he had come to accept as a result of his experiences at sea, during the protest march and whilst he was in jail. He also accepted Charles Darwin's idea of the survival of the fittest believing that the best way to survive hardships was through adapting.

Even though he felt that everyone should have a fair chance in life once he heard about the discovery of gold in Alaska from people disembarking (30) a sailing ship in San Francisco docks in 1897 Jack decided that if he could get rich quickly he would be able to give up manual work and concentrate on writing.

So in September after borrowing money for his supplies Jack boarded a steamship and began his two month long, 4,800 kms (3,000 mile) voyage to the town of Dawson, Canada by sea, river and on foot. The winter of 1897-8 arrived early and Jack was forced to live in a disused cabin with some other prospectors until the spring arrived. He eventually took over a plot of land on which to search for gold but he only ever panned (31) a tiny amount of gold worth $4.50.

Jack had hardly eaten any fruit or vegetables since leaving California and by the summer of 1899 he had severe scurvy, was very weak and had lost four teeth. Fresh food was scarce and very expensive and after a priest had given him some potatoes as a one-off gift he was advised to return home if he wanted to survive.

So Jack and a friend decided to pilot a rowing boat 3,000 kms (2,000 miles) westwards along the Yukon River until they reached the port of St. Michael where Jack caught a steamship back to San Francisco 6,500 kms (4,000 miles) away paying for his journey by shovelling coal to feed the ship's boilers.

Although he had not made his fortune he had benefited from wide range of experiences that he would use later for his stories. Sadly his stepfather had died during his absence and so once again his family were dependent on Jack for money.

As a result Jack decided that writing lots of short stories, as the Jungle Book author Rudyard Kipling had done, would be the quickest way to earn money and become famous and so he began writing stories about his adventures. New technologies were now available which made it cheap to print magazines and so very suddenly magazine publishers needed the sort of adventure stories that Jack was capable of writing.

On 7th April 1900, the same day that his book The Son of the Wolf was published Jack married Elizabeth ("Bessie") Maddern, a teacher who had helped to prepare him for his University of California entrance exam. He made it clear that he wasn't marrying her out of love but out of friendship and in the hopes that they would be able to have children and although Bessie did have two girls their marriage did not last and they divorced in 1904.

In October 1902 Jack travelled to England to work as a newspaper reporter. However, when the job that he was promised was cancelled Jack chose to stay in London and to investigate the hardships suffered by working class people in the East End, just as Charles Dickens had done before him, eventually publishing a book entitled The People of the Abyss (1903).

In 1904 he spent six months as a newspaper reporter in China and Korea writing about the Russian-Japanese War and although he was arrested "for spying" on several occasions he was able to obtain his release because he had influential American friends who were diplomats (32). On his return to the US he used his experiences and his notes to produce some fictional work, including A Nose for the King (1904) and The Star Rover (1914) which he could not have written without his war experiences.

By 1906 his name and his writing were recognised across America and by the time he was in his late 20s he had written eight books including his classic: The Call of the Wild & Typhoon (1903)

On his return from Korea he fell in love with Charmian Kittredge, the woman who eventually became his second wife, and they set up home together on a 1,000 acre ranch north of San Francisco. Charmian hoped that this would help him to settle down.

Jack however, was like a butterfly and for this reason he and Charmian made several long voyages to Hawaii and Australia on an expensive yacht that he had had specially built for them, leaving his staff to take care of their ranch. Subsequently he gave lectures and wrote stories based upon his visits.

However, his urge to fit in everything that he wanted to do with the remainder of his life caused him a great deal of stress and he developed various illnesses which he attempted to treat himself, usually wrongly. Some of his illnesses were real and some imagined but either way Jack also did a lot of damage to his body through drinking too much alcohol.

As he became iller and and less able to sleep he started to think more about his behaviour and he realised that he needed to be more self-controlled. However, he wasn't very successful at self discipline, a failure that he wrote about in his two autobiographical books: Martin Eden (1909) and John Barleycorn (1913).

His reluctance to ask his doctor for help led to a serious deterioration in his health and he died on his ranch just before his forty-first birthday.

However, at least his 'cat with nine lives' (33) existence had enabled him to write over fifty very popular books, many people believing some of his short stories to be his best work. Between 1878-2020 his publications in 55 languages is calculated to have been 30,721.

Several geographical features are named after him including Mount London in British Columbia in Canada and Jack London Lake in the Yagodninsky district of Magadan Oblast, Far Eastern Russia. Jack London Square, Oakland, California is also named in his honour.

> *"I would rather be a superb meteor, every atom of me in magnificent glow, than a sleepy and permanent planet."*
>
> J. London

E. B. White

(a.k.a. Elwyn Brooks White)

- **Life span:** 11 July 1899 - 1 October 1985
- **Born:** Mount Vernon, New York City, U.S.A.
- **First book:** The Lady is Cold and Other Poems (1929)

Elwyn White was the youngest in his family, his parents' sixth child. His father Samuel was a piano manufacturer and his mother Jessie was the family homemaker (1) who also raised chickens in their garden. Elwyn who was called "En" at home had three sisters and two brothers but it was his brother Stan, eight years older than him, who helped En to explore nature and to learn to read.

Although his father earned an adequate salary there was never a great deal of money to spare and all the children attended local state schools. During the last part of World War 1 En served as a soldier in France for a short period after which he attended Cornell University in New York State between 1919-1921 to study English. While he was there he accepted the nickname Andy because of a tradition that all male students named White were automatically nicknamed Andy in honour of the university's co-founder Andrew White.

He took on the editor's role of the university newspaper and because of his love of creative writing, despite being offered a teaching job in the University of Minnesota after graduating, he turned the job down because he wanted to become a writer.

Instead he drove to the other side of the USA with a friend and accepted a job with a newspaper in Seattle. Then after a year as a reporter he worked as a cabin boy on a steamboat that plied various Alaskan and arctic sea routes.

When he returned to New York he spent two years working as a production assistant and copywriter (34) for an advertising company and it was during this period that some of his poems were published in The New Yorker magazine.

Once he had he had secured a permanent job with The New Yorker in 1927 he wrote hundreds of articles and poems for it. His writing was so clear, thoughtful and amusing that many people believed that he was largely responsible for the success of the magazine, one which was considered the best weekly magazine in the USA at that time.

Not long afterwards En fell in love with Katherine Angell, the magazine's fiction editor and once she was divorced they married in 1927.

Besides writing lots of material for the magazine White also wrote a number of novels and collections of poetry for adults. However, it was his children's books commencing with Stuart Little (1945) that made him popular with families.

Once, whilst he was travelling on a night-train he dreamt about a 5 cm (2 inch) tall boy who is born into an ordinary family but who looked like a mouse. The tiny but mature mouse-boy behaved like a human teenager and proved that he could live in the normal world. Stuart's Little's parents were not worried that their son had been born a mouse and the object of En's story was to encourage anyone who considered themselves odd or different to accept themselves.

Charlotte's Web (1952) was published next and concerned a piglet who experienced the rejection of other animals and even faced death. The piglet was befriended by a spider who used its web to display messages that caused certain human beings to think more carefully about killing the pig for a Christmas meal. Fern, a little girl in the story learns about responsibility by caring for the piglet and she also learns that she can make a difference in the world by standing up for what she believes in. The author also used the friendship between the piglet and the spider to show that despite their physical differences they could learn to tolerate each other. The piglet also learns to cope with fear, loss, death and loneliness.

The Trumpet of the Swan (1970), En's version of The Ugly Duckling story, was his final children's book. It concerns the story of a swan called Louis who despite being born without a voice overcomes this difficulty by becoming a trumpet player to compensate for his lack of a natural 'voice' and to impress Serena, a beautiful swan. He is helped by his swan father who steals a trumpet for him and by Sam Beaver, an 11-year-old human friend. Finally Louis is able to attract a mate and eventually they fly away together.

Although it is 50 years since he wrote his final story all his stories are still very popular and his first two books have been adapted into films, television series and plays. 255 editions of Stuart Little were published between 1945-2018 in 12 languages and 462 editions of Charlotte's Web were published between 1952-2019 in 23 languages.

Both children and adults have appreciated his writing and he has been awarded numerous awards, medals and memberships of important organisations.

He was however, a very shy man who preferred to stand back from life's busyness in order to be able to observe things more clearly and to write about them. In 1963 and 1971 he even apologised for failing to attend two award ceremonies during which he was to receive the Presidential Medal of Freedom and National Medal for Literature.

White died in 1985 with his second wife outliving him by 7 years.

"Always be on the lookout for the presence of wonder."
E.B. White

Theodor Seuss Geisel

(a.k.a. Dr. Seuss)

- **Life span:** 2 March 1904 – 24 September 1991
- **Born:** Springfield, Massachusetts, U.S.A.
- **First book:** The Seven Lady Godivas (1939).

Dr Suess wasn't a doctor. In real life he was a poet, a writer, an illustrator, a cartoonist, an animator (35) and a filmmaker. His books for children generally combined imaginative characters and rhymes.

His grandparents were German immigrants and because his mother's maiden name (36) was Suess (pronounced 'zoyce' rhyming with voice) he adopted Dr Suess as his pen-name. He also wrote more than a dozen books using the pen name Theo LeSieg (i.e. his surname spelt backwards) and a further book using the pen name Rosetta Stone.

Because his family were of German descent, Theo (who was also called Ted) and his sister 'Marnie' suffered a lot of anti-German name-calling and bullying by other children when World War I began. Their father Theodor was the manager of their family brewery but later, when it had to close because of prohibition laws (37) he became the manager of all the parks in Springfield. Henrietta, their mother who was the family homemaker (1) used to sing rhymes at bedtime, something that encouraged him to create rhymes later on.

He graduated from High School in 1921 to study for a B.A. degree (38) at Dartmouth College where he became the editor-in-chief of the college's comedy magazine. Once however, he was made to resign from all his non-educational college activities because he was discovered attending a party where alcohol was being served. However, despite this ban he craftily continued working for the magazine by using the name Seuss.

In 1925 Seuss attended Oxford University, England to study for a Master's degree in literature (39) where he met Helen Pamer who later became his wife. He didn't however, complete his degree course. This was partly because Helen persuaded him to concentrate on a drawing career. Helen was also a successful children's author but she gave her up own career to focus on his work and she acted as his editor, spokesperson and financial adviser.

Following his return to the USA he became a copywriter (34) and an artist for magazines. He was so successful and earned so much money during the Great

Depression (40) that by 1936 he and his wife had been able to afford to visit over 30 different countries for pleasure while many other Americans were starving.

In 1939 he published his first book for adults. However, it wasn't very successful and he decided he would focus on children's books instead introducing a mixture of humour and the playful use of words, rhymes and outlandish characters.

Geisel also assisted the U.S. army during World War II by making training films for soldiers and by producing political cartoons for newspapers. However, once the war ended the couple moved to California and he resumed writing children's books.

In 1954, after an educational publisher challenged him to create a book for children who were not progressing very well with their reading he wrote The Cat in the Hat to help them learn the 250 words that were considered most important for 6-7 year olds. It's blend of verse, rhymes, pictures and humour made it a huge success both in America and internationally. In fact 286 editions of it were published between 1955 – 2018 in 10 languages, something that motivated him to write more than sixty more books for early learners and young children during his life.

On several other occasions however, he drew cartoons for magazines that were hostile towards black Americans and Japanese-American citizens (41). He did however, apologise for these later.

His views about right and wrong could be very changeable; for example he wrote about the Lorax who spoke up for a forest because "trees have no tongues" and also about the Grinch who finally realised that Christmas was about so much more than glitz and gifts. However, he also caused his very sick wife a great deal of unhappiness when he fell in love with his neighbour. Sadly his wife died in 1967 allowing Suess to marry Audrey one year later.

Audrey realised however, that marrying Giesel was going to mean huge changes for her and her family and she even arranged for her two daughters to be sent to boarding school to please her new husband.

During his 23 year long second marriage he wrote another 48 children's books including You're Only Old Once! (1986) and his last book Oh, the Places You'll Go! (1990) that was published the year before his death.

As one of the most popular children's authors of all time, Geisel's 60 books have topped most children's bestseller lists and sold over 222 million copies, many in more than 15 languages. Although famous for his books he also released a large number of cartoons, films, tv series, video-cassettes and video games.

In 2004, he won the USA's annual Theodor Seuss Geisel Award for the most distinguished book published in English for beginners in 2003.

Dr. Seuss's honours include two Academy Awards, two Emmy Awards, a Peabody Award, a Laura Ingalls Wilder Medal, an Inkpot Award and a special Pulitzer Prize for his contribution to the education and enjoyment of America's children and their parents during the previous 50 years.

Until her death his wife continued to help with turning his creations into various Suess products and even today his work continues to help millions of children around the world to read.

"If things start happening – don't worry –
just keep going and you'll start happening too."
T. Gielsel

Beverly Atlee Cleary

(born Beverly Atlee Bunn)

- **Life span:** 12 April 1916 – 25 April 2021
- **Born:** McMinnville, Oregon, U.S.A.
- **First book:** Henry Huggins (1942)

Beverly Bunn, the only child of a farmer and his school teacher wife lived with her parents on their farm in Yamhill County, Oregon. However, when she was 6 years old they moved to Portland, Oregon after her father accepted a job as a bank security guard. This was during the time of The Great Depression (40) that had led to the failure of their family farm.

Beverly found life and school much more difficult in a city and she struggled to learn to read. She was particularly disappointed to discover that lots of the books for young children, many of which were published in England, were about characters in rich families who had nannies and ponies.

Fortunately, a school librarian was able to introduce her to a few other books and by age of 8 or 9 years she was a good reader having caught up with the others in her class. When she was 11 or 12 her creative writing so impressed her teacher that the teacher suggested that she might think about becoming a children's writer later. Cleary attended Grant High School in Portland, Oregon and Chaffey College in Alta Loma, California during which time she made a plan to become a children's librarian.

Between 1934-38 she studied for a B.A. degree (38) in English at the University of California, Berkeley although she also had to do part-time work to pay her fees. She also met her future husband Clarence Cleary there. Her part-time jobs included working as a seamstress (42) and a chambermaid. In 1939, after working with children as part of another course she graduated from the University of Washington with a M.A. degree (39) in Library Science and worked for a year as a children's librarian. She also worked for a time as a librarian in an army hospital. Her parents didn't want her to marry a Roman Catholic man and so in 1940 she and Clarence eloped (43).

At the end of World War II she and her husband settled in Carmel-by-the-Sea, California where their twins were born.

It was not until she was 29 years old however, that she began working full-time as a children's writer, publishing her first book "Henry Huggins" in 1950. This was the first in a series of chapter books about Henry, his dog, a neighbourhood friend and her little sister Ramona. This was the first of many stories about ordinary people living ordinary lives based on Cleary's own experiences of children growing up in her neighbourhood, as well as her work with children whom she met whilst working as a librarian.

In 1950 she began to publish her Henry Huggins series followed by in her Ramona Quimby series in 1955. Gradually she introduced more humour into her stories in order to increase the enjoyment of her readers and to motivate them to read more.

She kept her writing simple and often included advice that her mum had given her. In particular she wrote about the sort of ordinary experiences that she believed most human beings faced.

In fact some people believe that she was one of the first American children's authors to describe her characters' true emotions, including those of children from middle-class families. In other words she was one of America's first "reality writers" (44). For example, in 1956 she published Fifteen in her First Love series. This was romantic novel aimed at helping teenagers to think about boy-girl relationships. In 1983 she published Dear Mr Henshaw as a result of several boys asking her to write a story about a boy whose parents had divorced.

Her books are said to have encouraged millions of children at times when they have felt confused or frightened, helping them to understand what to expect from life. She was always been respectful of her fictional characters and none of them were allowed to laugh at anyone else.

She was one of America's most successful authors and she published over 40 books before retiring in 2000. She sold more than 90 million copies of her books in more than 20 different languages. In 1988 Canadian TV created a 10 part series which followed the life of eight-year-old Ramona Quimby and then, in 2010, a movie Ramona and Beezus, was released. New editions of Henry Huggins; The Mouse and the Motorcycle and Ramona Quimby, Age 8 were released in January 2016 to celebrate Cleary's 100th birthday.

Cleary also wrote two memoirs (45), A Girl from Yamhill (1988) and My Own Two Feet (1995).

Clearly collected an enormous number of awards and in addition a couple of statues of her famous characters were erected in Portland. Also two Portland schools that she attended were renamed after her, i.e. her former elementary school in 1995 and Fernwood Grammar School in 2008.

During her life time she gained many awards and lots of recogition. For example in 2004 The University of Washington Information School finished fund-raising to pay for a professor's salary each year. This award is named The Beverly Cleary Endowed Chair for Children and Youth Services and it honours her work and commitment to librarianship. The Beverly Cleary Hall, a residential accommodation building at The University of California, Berkeley, is also named in her honour.

She died in California at the age of 104, 17 years after her husband.

A day known as "D.E.A.R. Day" (Drop Everything and Read Day) is celebrated in the U.S.A. each year on her former birthday.

"When I was a librarian boys in particular asked me where they could they find books about kids like them. However, there weren't any."
B. Clearly

Madeleine L'Engle Camp

(pronounced Leng-el Camp)

- **Life span:** 29 November 1918 –
  6 September 2007
- **Birthplace:** New York, U.S.A.
- **First book:** The Small Rain (1945)

Charles, her father, was 39 years old when Madeleine, his first and only child, was born and his wife was 37 years old. As a result, and because they hadn't had children to care for during the previous twenty years, they found it difficult to give their daughter the time and emotional closeness that she needed as an infant.

Her father was a drama and music critic for a newspaper and her mother, who was also called Madeleine, was a concert pianist. This led to them being very busy people and as a result when her parents were entertaining guests at home Madeleine had to sit quietly on the sidelines watching and listening. However, her parents employed a very kind and cheerful Irish Catholic housekeeper who helped them to care for Madeleine.

As a young child she spent hours alone in her bedroom reading and day dreaming. In particular she loved the Anne of Green Gables series by L. M. Montgomery, Frances Hodgson Burnett's The Secret Garden and E. Nesbit's books, including The Railway Children. In fact it was not long before she began writing her own stories and poems.

Her parents had very different ideas about how and where she should be educated which resulted in her being taught by various governesses and later on in different schools. Madeleine felt that some of her teachers and fellow students treated her as though she was stupid and unimportant, so much so that she retreated into reading and writing on her own in order to cope with her feelings.

She entered a poetry contest when she about 10 years old and won it. However, her teachers couldn't believe she had written it which resulted in her mother having to prove that her daughter was indeed talented by showing them some of her other writing.

She enjoyed her time at the Todhunter School in New York, a private school for upper-class girls although at the age of 12 she was transferred to Chablard School, an expensive girls' boarding school in Switzerland. This was because her parents had been advised to move there for the sake of her father's ill health. This transfer left her feeling abandoned by her parents and she came to hate her boarding school life. She also felt rejected by the other girls and as a result she spent long periods in a silent fantasy world in which she created stories.

Three years later however, the family moved back to the U.S.A. and just before her 15th birthday Madeleine was sent to Ashley Hall Boarding School, Charleston, South Carolina. Although this was 400 kms (250 miles) away from her parents' home in Florida she liked the new school more and after joining the drama club she began to love acting and writing plays.

Four years later, and a year after her father's death, Madeleine began studying for a B.A. degree (38) in English literature at Smith College in Northampton, Massachusetts. Whilst she was attending it she also wrote material for its newspaper and its journals. It was at this point that she added L'Engle, her second Christian name, to her surname so that her published writing would not be confused with her father's.

After graduating in 1942 she moved back to New York where she met the man who later become her husband. Hugh Franklin was an actor and the two of them enjoyed acting together in theatres. Madeleine even managed to write two books whilst they were on tour making enough money to rent an apartment in Greenwich Village, New York by doing both things.

They were married in 1946 and Josephine their first child was born in 1947 when Madeleine was 29 years old. At first they continued to live in New York but once they began earning less money because Madeleine was no longer able to look after a toddler and write books at the same time they decided to move to Goshen, Connecticut. There they bought a 200 year old house and a small shop which her husband ran. Meanwhile L'Engle Camp continued with her writing. Their son Bion was also born at this time, i.e. in 1952.

As she approached her 40th birthday and because she had only managed to get one book published during the previous 6-7 years she considered giving up writing. However, whilst they were on a family camping holiday some fresh ideas came into her head and she began to write her most famous book: A Wrinkle in Time.

When she was 41 they returned to live in New York and although she was a teacher at St. Hilda's & St. Hugh's Elementary School in Manhattan for several long periods she also managed to complete her masterpiece by 1960. The manuscript for her book however, which has been called "one of the great American novels of the 20th century" was rejected more than thirty times before it was finally published in 1962.

Once they were living in to New York again not only did her husband start working again as an actor but in 1965 Madeleine began to work as a voluntary librarian in the Roman Catholic Cathedral of St. John the Divine in Manhattan. She used the quiet surroundings of its library for her writing and she also became a very popular listener and advisor to those people who sought her help. In fact she spent almost 30 years helping there.

As a writer with a strong Christian faith many of her stories have been described as being equally as good as the Narnia stories by C.S. Lewis. However, some of her critics have disliked her links between between fantasy, Christianity, myths and witchcraft. Other readers however, have been fascinated by her use of some of the scientific material that she absorbed during her research. The former NASA astronaut Dr Janice Voss, for example, said once that the book A Wrinkle in Time helped her to decide to becoming an astronaut.

During the 1960s, 70s and 80s, L'Engle Camp wrote dozens of books, lots of poetry and a number of plays for children and adults that often crossed several genres. Not only did she use scientific and religious imagery in her writing but she also introduced her strong belief in the healing power of love, particularly the love shared between family members.

In addition to the numerous awards, medals and prizes that she earned she was also awarded 17 honorary (46) degrees by various universities. Her work was recognised by the World Fantasy Convention too, in 1997, when she received a Lifetime Achievement Award and in 2011, several years after her death, she was inducted into the New York Writers' Hall of Fame.

Frequently blending fantasy, science and Christianity together L'Engle Camp's output was as varied as it was prolific. Not only did she write more than 25 novels, short stories and picture books for adults, teenagers and children but her published work also included three books about religion for adults, three books of prayers and more than half a dozen non-fiction books, including her Crosswicks Journals, a memoir series in which she shared her thinking about creativity, family, and faith.

During the period 1944 – 2020 she produced 2,950 publications in 15 languages and between 1962 – 2019 her book: A Wrinkle in Time was produced in 422 different editions in 15 languages. In addition a film version of her book A Ring of Endless Light (1980) was released in 2002 plus two film versions of her book A Wrinkle in Time (1962) in 2003 and 2018.

She spent the last few years of her life living in a nursing home in Connecticut and died of natural causes at the age of 83, 15 years after her husband.

"A child will come with an open mind, whereas many adults come to an open book with a closed mind".

M. L'Engle Camp

Richard McClure Scarry

- **Life span:** 5 June 1919 – 30 April 1994
- **Born:** Boston, Massachusetts, U.S.A.
- **First book Illustrated:** Two Little Miners (1949) by M. Wise Brown & E. Thacher Hurd

Richard was the second of five children born to Mary and John James Scarry. Richard's father owned Scarry's Department Store, a large clothing store in Field's Corner, Dorchester, Massachusetts.

Young Richard was not an outstanding pupil in school and because he often paid more attention to the worms and insects that he smuggled into the classroom than to his lessons he was frequently sent out to stand in the school corridor! In fact, it took him an extra year to achieve the necessary grades to graduate from High School.

Although Richard's father enrolled his son in Boston's Business School after Richard had spent a dreary year there, it was agreed that he should instead study drawing and painting at the Boston Museum School of Fine Arts.

When the United States entered the Second World War, Richard was conscripted (53) into the Army. He was eventually sent to the Allied Forces Headquarters in Algiers where he worked as an editor and illustrator, writing news articles and manuals for the troops, drawing maps and designing posters.

Once the war was over, Richard went to New York and began looking for work as an illustrator for magazines. His career as a children's book illustrator began with a commission (50) to illustrate a number of titles in the Little Golden Books series, a new line of more affordable storybooks.

In 1949 he met his future wife, Patricia Murphy, a Canadian. She was a copywriter (34) at Young and Rubicam, a large advertising agency. "Patsy" was equally good at writing charming stories and soon Patsy was writing Little Golden Books which Richard would then illustrate.

Danny Beaver's Secret (1953), Pierre Bear (1954), and The Bunny Book (1955) were some of the books that they published as a result of their teamwork.

In 1951 the Scarrys moved to Ridgefield, Connecticut, where they rented a small cottage on a farm. This same year, Richard wrote and illustrated his first book:

The Great Big Car and Truck Book. Their son, Richard II, "Huck", was born in 1953.

In 1958, the family moved to a seaside house in Westport, Connecticut, an hour's train journey away from his publisher's office.

Richard wrote a great many books during the 1960s including numerous large-format books. These included: The Best Word Book Ever (1963), Busy, Busy World (1965), Storybook Dictionary (1966) and What Do People Do All Day? (1968).

The Scarry's loved to travel and as a result of having visited Europe on a number of previous occasions Richard decided that they would spend the whole of 1968 in Europe. This allowed them to improve their French and to explore other countries. They settled in the city of Lausanne, Switzerland which was very close to some excellent places for skiing, a sport which Richard adored.

Although they had not planned to stay in Switzerland for any longer than a year, in fact the Scarry's never returned to live on the North American continent.

Richard produced many popular books during the 1970s and 1980s, his illustrations frequently reflecting the buildings around him, whether in towns or near the ski slopes.

In 1972, Richard purchased a small chalet in the village of Gstaad for use during weekends and as a result he was able to ski even more often. He could even walk to the ski lifts from his front door. Soon their weekends in the mountains grew longer until the family no longer returned to Lausanne for the start of each working week, allowing them more time to work and play in Gstaad, the village that they had come to love.

Books that he wrote during this period include: The Great Pie Robbery (1968), Supermarket Mystery (1968), Great Big Schoolhouse (1968), Funniest Storybook Ever (1972), Cars and Trucks and Things That Go! (1974), and The Biggest Word Book Ever (1985).

Millions of children around the world have come to love the crowded, busy and funny scenes in Busytown, inhabited by such characters as Huckle Cat and Lowly Worm and as a result of them feeling secure with his humanised animal characters, huge numbers of children have Richard to thank for helping them to begin to learn to read.

Well over 100 million of his books have been sold and many of them have been translated into other languages, i.e. more than 25 different ones.

Although his work has at times been criticised for not being sophisticated, he never felt the need to change his style. After all, he had millions of readers who simply loved his books.

His characters and books have been adapted for television and produced as videos and DVDs and in addition, a great many Busytown toys and games have also been created, produced and sold.

Richard suffered a heart attack in 1994 and died in Saanen, Switzerland at the age of 75. His wife Patsy died the following year.

In 2010, or around that time, Richard received a "lifetime achievement" award from the New York Society of Illustrators in recognition of his work.

"I'm not interested in creating a book that is read once and then placed on a shelf and forgotten. I am happiest when people have worn-out my books, and they are held together with Scotch tape."
Richard Scarry

Maurice Bernard Sendak

- **Life span:** 10 June 1928 – 8 May 2012.
- **Birthplace:** Brooklyn, New York, U.S.A.
- **First book:** Kenny's Window (1956)

Maurice's parents were a Jewish couple who moved from Poland in 1913 and who got married in Brooklyn. Until his business collapsed during The Great Depression (40) his father Philip was a dressmaker and his mother Sarah was the family homemaker. They had three children. When Maurice was born his sister Natalie was nine, and his brother Jack was five.

Their father was a colourful storyteller who would often tell his children scary tales that he made up spontaneously which he could spread over several nights. Maurice suffered a series of illnesses before he started school, including smallpox, diphtheria (17), measles and pneumonia. These meant him having spend to a lot of time either in bed or in the family kitchen with his mother and grandmother.

When he was 6 years old and his brother was 11 they wrote a book together about the value of siblings remaining close to each other and it was around this time that Maurice realised that he wanted to write and illustrate stories.

It may have been his obsession with Mickey Mouse and the Disney film Fantasia at the age of 12 that made him decide to become an illustrator but he also said that he was very influenced by his Jewish background; by Herman Melville, the writer of Moby Dick; by the poet Emily Dickinson and by the composer Mozart.

Sendak loathed school because he hated the noise and commotion. Also, because he was physically frail he was bullied and he was unable to join in with many of the activities and sports either. Between 1941-45, he attended Brooklyn's enormous Lafayette High School along with 4,499 other students where his dislike of school continued except for during art lessons.

After leaving school at the age of 18 Maurice gathered his artwork together and began searching for a job in which he could use his artistic talents. His skills were soon recognised and he found a job designing shop window displays. He kept this job for three years during which time he developed his skills and artistic style by designing layouts for shop windows by day and by attending art lessons in the evenings.

By the time he was in his 20s his skills had developed so well that a book publisher offered to pay him to illustrate other authors' books. However, once he had begun to illustrate and publish his own stories, commencing with Very Far Away (1956) his popularity sky-rocketed. In 1963, when he was 35 years old Sendak created Where the Wild Things Are, a book that would eventually become a favourite tale for millions of children and adults in America, Europe and Asia. 587 editions of this were published between 1963-2020 in 17 languages.

In 1964, at the halfway point of his artistic career, he received a Caldecott Medal, the highest award for children's books for that book, after which he accepted another 40 or more commissions (50) for book illustrations, as well as writing and illustrating at least another dozen of his own stories. In 1976 he won another Caldecott Medal, this time for his fantasy story In the Night Kitchen (1970).

Between 1965-2005 Sendak also spent a great deal of time designing stage sets and costumes for opera houses, ballet companies, music festivals and television and film studios. At the same time he continued to illustrate books by other authors, two examples being Zlateh the Goat and Other Stories (1966) by Isaac Bashevis Singer and The Singing Family of the Cumberlands (1980) by Jean Richielong.

In 1972, Maurice and his close friend Eugene Glynn moved to Ridgefield, Connecticut where he continued his work.

In 1981, Sendak finished the book that he considered his best work, Outside Over There, a creation that he said was inspired by his older sister who looked after him when their mother was at work.

Sendak's final book: My Brother's Book (2013), published a long time after his brother's death in 1995, was a tribute to his brother and to "others we love who have already died" including perhaps his friend of 50 years standing, Eugene?

Following his death The New York Times newspaper called Sendak "the most important children's artist of the 20th century." For example 590 editions of his book Where the Wild Things Are were published between 1963 – 2020 in 17 languages.

Presumably such praise would not have come as any surprise to him in view of all the recognition that he had already received? In 1996, Sendak was awarded a National Medal of Arts as a writer, illustrator and designer, followed in 2003 by an Astrid Lindgren Memorial Award for children's literature.

After he died in Connecticut at the age of 83 two primary schools – one in North Hollywood and the other in Brooklyn, New York – were named in his honour.

> *"You can't write for children. They're much too complicated.*
> *You can only write books that may be of interest to them."*
> M. B. Sendak

Eric Carle

- **Life span:** 25 June 1929 – 23 May 2021
- **Birthplace:** Syracuse, New York State
- **First book:** 1, 2, 3 to the Zoo (1968)

Carle's parents Erich and Johanna were a young German couple who moved to New York State in 1928 seeking "a better life". When Eric was a little boy his father used to take him on nature walks during which they talked about the insects, plants and birds they spotted. Also, because his dad was an amateur artist, the two of them used to make up stories and draw together. His mother though according to Eric, was not a very warm person emotionally.

Eric enjoyed his time at primary school and in particular drawing and painting. His teacher mentioned these skills to his mother and suggested that she should encourage him with these.

In 1935 because Eric's mother was missing her home in Germany the family moved back to Stuttgart. Her husband owned a four-storey house in which more than a dozen members of this large family lived together.

The rules in German schools were much harsher and Eric was once caned on both hands for doing something wrong. Also, because he was small and underweight for his age he was sent to a health camp for periods of time where he was encouraged to eat more. He became used to being away from his home and he spent many of his summer holidays on farms owned by relatives or friends helping out as well drawing animals and insects. In particular he loved his Uncle August who was an artist and a storyteller and from whom from whom Eric would beg stories.

Art was the only subject that Eric enjoyed at secondary school and when his art teacher noticed his more relaxed style of drawing and painting he introduced Eric to the paintings of some famous 20th century artists. Eric had never seen paintings by artists such as Picasso, Matisse, Kandinsky before and he fell in love with their artistic styles and colours.

Sadly however, the enjoyment of painting and drawing that Eric and his father had shared came to a end when his father was sent to Russia as part of the German army during World War II. When his father returned home 8 years later his physical and his emotional health had deteriorated drastically as result of his experiences.

When Eric was 14 yrs old the British Royal Air Force was bombing Stuttgart so heavily that most children were evacuated to the countryside near the German-Swiss border and later he was forced to help to dig trenches alongside the River Rhine that German soldiers would be able to fight from were the war to get any worse. However, none of the people who were compelled to dig these ditches, including other teenagers, prisoners war and slave labourers were fed properly and when they was rescued by American and English soldiers at the end of the war they were extremely thin and hungry. Also, when Eric returned to Stuttgart his house, whose roof, front door and windows had been destroyed, was the only building that remained standing on his street.

Eric returned to secondary school and soon afterwards he asked his art teacher to suggest an art-related job that might suit him and somewhere where he would be able to study. His teacher suggested that he should study commercial art at Stuttgart's Academy of Visual Art and even though he wasn't officially old enough he managed to begin studying there at 16 years of age.

However, because his artwork was not as good as that of the other students he was transferred to another class to study typography (51). Although this was not his first choice Carle said later that what he learned there helped him in the graphic design work (52) that he studied before he leaving the Academy.

After four years of study Carle got a job as a graphic designer with the U.S.A. Information Service in Germany designing propaganda (48) posters aimed at convincing German people that the American way of life was something worth seeking.

He had always wanted to return to America and in 1952 with only a small amount of money in his pocket he found work as graphic designer with The New York Times newspaper. However, four months later his work was interrupted when he was conscripted (53) into the U.S. army and sent back to Germany where he was worked in the U.S. Army Postal Service until 1956. In 1953 he married his first wife in Stuttgart and they had two children. Then, once he had completed his military service they returned to the USA where he continued to work for The New York Times.

After two years he became the art director of an agency in New York that produced advertising artwork for drug manufacturing companies. However, after four years he got fed up with having to travel to different parts of the world to attend meetings and so in 1963 he decided to become a freelance (49) graphic designer and illustrator.

It wasn't however, until the mid 1960s that he began to become well-known. A friend of his saw a collage (54) of a red lobster that Carle had created for a drug advertisement and he was asked to illustrate a picture book called Brown Bear, Brown Bear, What Do You See? (1967). This was when Eric decided to become a children's author and illustrator.

He was not very confident about his creative writing skills at first and so he began by producing 1, 2, 3 to the Zoo (1968), a book for pre-school children without words.

Carle once explained that with his books he was attempting to create bridges between the security that a child feels at home and the unknown world that he or she meets at school and to show them that learning can be fascinating and enjoyable.

His next, and most famous project, was originally going to be about a book-munching green worm. However, although his editor liked his idea she suggested that children would prefer a caterpillar. Eric loved her idea and decided that although it wouldn't be biologically true-to-life he would show his butterfly emerging from a cocoon instead of from a chrysalis. He did this, he explained, because he remembered his dad repeatedly encouraging him to come out of his self-protective cocoon and to be more open to the world around him. Thus this fictionalised version was published rather than a factually correct account of the life cycle of a butterfly.

It has been estimated that 829 editions of this book have been produced between 1969 – 2020 in 19 languages and has sold more than 50 million copies, i.e. nearly two copies every minute. In addition to this one he has also illustrated more than seventy others, most of which he also wrote. More than 145 million copies of his books have been sold around the world.

In 2002 he and his wife founded The Eric Carle Museum of Picture Book Art next to Hampshire College, Amherst, Massachusetts.

In 2019 to honour his work and because his love of insects a previously unknown spider was named Uroballus Carlei in his honour. During his lifetime however, he also received a lot more recognition and a great many awards.

He remained married to his first wife for six years and they raised a son and daughter together. However, in 1973 he married his second wife Barbara, a special needs teacher from North Carolina, who died in 2015.

"I often remind people to remember the four magic letters: DO & IT."

E. Carle

Robert Munsch

(a.k.a. Robert Norman Peter Maria Munsch)

- Life span: 11th June 1945 – present
- Born: Pittsburgh, Pennsylvania, USA
- First book: Mud Puddle (1979)

Robert, who became known as Bob, was the fourth of nine children in a Roman Catholic family. His father Thomas was a lawyer and his mother Margaret was the family homemaker. As a young child Robert had an imaginary friend named Bobby Smith who was very naughty. Bob struggled at junior school and at the age of 11 he was still using his fingers to help him to do sums. Although he wasn't very good at spelling either he wrote lots of silly and funny poems at junior school. As an adult Bob once described himself as "like a very mature six-year-old." Science was Munsch's favourite subject at school and Charles Darwin was his hero. He also loved Dr Suess.

After finishing his secondary education he spent seven years preparing to become a Roman Catholic priest by studying for a B.A. degree (38) in history and a Master's degree (39) in anthropology (55) in two different universities. Next he studied for a second Master's degree in child development and early education.

In 1971 whilst he was a part-time worker in a childcare centre in Boston he met Ann, another childcare worker, and they were married the following year. Even though he had experience as a teacher and a headteacher he and his wife were actually working in a children's day care centre in 1975 when the money to pay their salaries ran out and it was at this point that they decided to move to Canada.

In Canada they found work in the University of Guelph, Ontario and they began studying child development in a university pre-school.

It was there that Bob's storytelling so impressed one of his colleagues that she encouraged him to write down some of his stories. At first he resisted this idea but when his boss gave him two months off to write up some of his stories he wrote a number of stories on the day before he was due to return to work and sent them off to ten different publishers. Each of the drafts were rejected except for Mud Puddle (1979) which went on to sell 3,000 copies in the first year. As a result of this success Munsch decided to quit his job as a pre-school children's worker and a researcher to focus on telling stories and writing.

Bob describes himself as an off-the-cuff (56) storyteller who uses over-emphasised expressions and different voices, seeing himself only secondarily as a writer.

His wife became pregnant twice although sadly both of their babies were stillborn (57). The couple were tremendously upset, so much so that Robert often drank a great deal alcohol to help him to cope with his sadness. Later though some very comforting words came into his mind: "I'll love you forever" .. and .. "as long as I'm living, my baby you'll be" and he would occasionally sing these words quietly to himself. In his way he was able to keep the memories alive of the babies that they might have had.

Later on he and his wife adopted three children. He also decided that he wanted to write a story to include those very special words. As a result he wrote Love You Forever, a book that has sold more than 23 million copies in North America.

Although the death of their two babies was an unusual subject for a children's book Bob has continued to use these sad events to stress the importance of not avoiding difficult subjects. For example, the main character in "Giant, or Waiting for the Thursday Boat" is a giant named McKeon who is angry at God and threatens to pound him into apple sauce.

In his 'story discussions' with children Munsch aims to talk about how his characters experience different emotions and about how they have coped with disabilities, bossy parents and other challenges, attempting at the same time to make kids feel that they are okay, that life isn't perfect and that everybody has challenges to deal with.

Neither has Munsch avoided discussing his own over-use of alcohol and drugs or his recovery from a stroke (10). He has also talked freely in the past about his bi-polar illness (58).

He prefers making up stories 'live' in front of children and basing the story he is creating upon the experiences of the child or children in his audience, naming the main character after one or some of them. Many people believe that his stories appeal to young children because he gives his characters power to question stereotypes (59) and to deal with the challenges they face tactfully, with bravery and humour.

It has been estimated that between 1945 – 2016 his work has included 4,128 publications in 15 languages. Some of Munsch's stories have been produced in drama and musicals and as television programmes and his Love You Forever words have been have been turned into a song.

In 1999 he was made a member of the Order of Canada, the country's second highest merit-based honour and in 2009 he was inducted into Canada's Walk of Fame. Whitby Primary School and Mount Albert Primary School, both in Ontario, have been renamed in his honour.

Robert lives in Guelph, Ontario, Canada with his wife.

"Those who have left gentle footprints on our hearts have left a story worth telling."
Anonymous.

Kathleen Margaret Pearson

(a.k.a. Kit Pearson)

- **Life span:** 30 April 1947 – present
- **Birthplace:** Edmonton, Alberta, Canada
- **First book:** The Daring Game (1986)

Kit's parents were 26 years old when Kit was born. Her father Sandy was a businessman and her mother Kay was the family homemaker. Two brothers were born later and the three children them were raised in Edmonton, central Canada during their early childhood.

Kit adored the different seasons, particularly the tranquil snowy winters and the warm blissful summers, and their peaceful home life suited Kit who was a quiet and timid child. She loved their dogs and she loved being read to.

She remembers being shy at school and at birthday parties but once she had learnt to read she was relieved to be able to escape into the world of books. She was also able to shelter in make-believe games whenever she felt frightened. In particular she remembers being afraid of things that she thought might have been under her bed.

When she was 8 years old however, her father's work meant them moving to Vancouver on the west coast 1,000 kms (700 miles) away. This was where they lived for the next four years and where she finally made two good friends. These were happy years in which she recalls all three of them acting out episodes from Robin Hood's life and stories of knights, of playing gods and goddesses, as well as enjoying the beautiful surroundings of this part of British Columbia.

This didn't last though because when she was 13 her family moved back to Edmonton leaving her very upset at the loss of her security and friends. However, once again books saved her and she buried herself in a variety of them including the Emily series by L.M. Montgomery, author of the Anne of Green Gables.

In fact the Emily books (1923-27) had such an impact on Kit that they made her decide that she would eventually become a writer. Creative writing however, was not something that she did much of in her primary school and because she had never met a writer or heard anyone talk about writing books the idea of becoming an author seemed so strange to her that she kept her ambition a secret.

When it was time for her to transfer to a secondary school she was sent back to Vancouver to attend a girls' boarding school. However, because Kit had been upset at losing contact with her girl friends in Vancouver several years earlier and because she had been lonely since her return to Edmonton she was pleased to return to a city about which she had such good memories. She made lots of new friends and as a result of falling in love with English literature at school she eventually transferred to study for a B.A degree (38) in English at Vancouver's University of British Columbia.

However, after a year her parents persuaded her to return to Edmonton and she continued her studies at the University of Alberta. Although she wasn't thrilled at being back in Edmonton she persisted with her course because she was enjoying the content of the course and it was during the last year of her studies, while she was still enjoying student life, that she began to wonder whether becoming a librarian might be a good career choice for her.

However, after graduating she spent time doing a number of different temporary jobs and visiting parts of Europe before beginning to study for a degree in librarianship at the University of British Columbia in Vancouver at the age of 28 years. Then, when she had finished her degree she moved to the Ontario 4,350 kms (2,700 miles) away to begin her first librarian's job in the city of St Catharines, close the US & Canadian border.

She didn't stay there very long though because of wanting to live nearer to friends and family members on that side of Canada and because of this she accepted a children's librarian's job in Toronto's North York Public Library 20 kms (12 miles away) where she stayed for next four years.

Working there made Kit even more determined to start writing children's books although she didn't actually begin doing this immediately. Instead she gave up being a librarian and began to study for a Master's degree (39) in children's literature at the The Centre for the Study of Children's Literature at Simmons College Boston, USA. This seemed to inspire her even more and as a result of encouragement from her teachers she found a part-time librarian's job nearer home and started writing a novel for children.

The result was her first book The Daring Game, a story focusing on girls attending a boarding school in the early 1960s, that was accepted by the third publishing company that she submitted it to.

Many of her stories take place in Canadian settings and in them Kit describes how the children felt and how they dealt with various difficult experiences and relationships involving other children and adults, many of whom were strangers.

Fortunately her books became so popular that she was quickly able to afford to reduce her working hours as a librarian. This also allowed her enough time to be able to give talks in schools and libraries and to teach adults about children's literature and about how to write for children.

To date Pearson has authored 12 books, two picture books and edited an anthology (60). Not only have some of these been translated into other languages but they have also appeared in other media formats.

Her work has been recognised through many awards including: a Mr. Christie's Book Award (1991), a Vlag en Wimpel prize (1992) for the Dutch edition of The Sky is Falling, a National I.O.D.E. Violet Downey Award (1994), a Vicky Metcalf Award (1998), a British Columbia Red Cedar Award (1999), two Ruth Schwartz Awards (1997 and 2012)

Kit was also awarded three Canadian Library Association Children's Book of the Year Awards in 1988, 1990 and 2012; two Geoffrey Bilson Awards for Historical Fiction in 1990 and 1994; two Manitoba Young Readers' Choice Awards in 1992 and 1997; a Governor-General's Literary award in 1997 and a Lieutenant Governor's Award for Literary Excellence in 2014. In addition, Kit was appointed to the Order of Canada in 2018, the country's second highest merit-based honour.

In 2005 and still very much in love with British Columbia Kit moved to live in the city of Victoria with her partner Katherine Farris. They have a small female labradoodle called Brio who shares their home and their lives.

"The more you read, the easier writing will become for you. It's hard to be disciplined at first but writing will eventually become a habit."

K. Pearson

David Murray Pilkey

(a.k.a. "Dav" Pilkey)

- **Life span:** 4th March 1966 – present
- **Born:** Cleveland, Ohio, U.S.A.
- **First book:** World War Won (1987)

The unusual spelling of Dav's Christian name came about as the result of the letter e being left off his name badge when he worked in a Pizza Hut restaurant. This spelling amused him and so he decided to carry on using it. However, he still pronounces his name 'Dave". Dav also wrote the Dumb Bunnies series of books but for these he used his pen name Sue Denim, a play on the word pseudonym.

His dad, David Pilkey, was a steel sales representative who later became a church minister and hospital chaplain (61) in Cleveland. His mother Barbara was the family homemaker (1) although she also used to play the organ in their church. His parents divorced when Dav and his older sister were at secondary school.

He spent a happy childhood in Elyria, Lorain County although he disliked outdoor games preferring instead to stay at home drawing animals, monsters and super-heroes.

At primary school he was the class clown and he became an expert at paper-ball spitting, throwing paper planes and making rude noises. In fact at the age of 6 he held the class record for cramming the most crayons up his nose at once. He had great difficulty in following the school's rules and he spent a lot of time sitting outside his classroom. It was on these occasions that he started developing his ideas about his Captain Underpants character.

Although Dav was eventually diagnosed with ADHD – Attention Deficit and Hyperactivity Disorder (62) – his mum and dad continued to be very patient with him and helped him to deal with all the criticism and bullying that he got at school. They also encouraged his drawing because this was one of his many strengths.

Dav prefers to call his ADHD "Attention Deficit and Hyperactivity Delight" because he has said that "giving someone an ADHD label doesn't prevent them from having fun or being creative."

He often reminds children that lots of well-known people struggled at school when they were younger including Albert Einstein, Thomas Edison, Keira Knightley, John Lennon and Muhammad Ali, all of whom became famous later.

After High School he went to Kent State University, Ohio to study English intending to become a teacher. However, one of the teachers noticed his cartoons and asked him if he had ever considered producing a children's book. As the result of her encouragement he wrote his first book and entered it into a national competition for student authors. He won the first prize in his age category, which resulted in him going on a trip to Kansas City to sign a publishing deal; something that marked the beginning of his writing and drawing career.

However, because no-one wanted to publish his next book he spent several years selling single copies of his book from the back of his car in order to earn enough money to live on and it took 23 rejections before his second book – 'Twas the Night Before Thanksgiving (1989) – was accepted by a publisher.

Since then Pilkey has written and illustrated many award winning series and stand-alone books. He is probably best known for his Captain Underpants series, his Dog Man graphic novel series and his "Cat Kid Comic Club" series. His Captain Underpants books have sold more than 80 million copies worldwide and have been translated into more than 28 languages.

In 2017, DreamWorks Animation brought his famous character to cinema screens in the film: Captain Underpants: The First Epic Movie and Netflix has streamed The Epic Tales of Captain Underpants as a TV show.

Awards that he has also earned include a Caldecott Honor Award in 1997 for The Paperboy; a California Young Reader Medal in 1998 for Dog Breath!: The Horrible Trouble with Hally Tosis; a Disney Adventures Kids' Choice Award in 2007 for his Captain Underpants series, a Milner Award in 2016 as Favourite Children's Author and in 2019 The Publishers' Weekly Person of the Year Award and the Comic Industry Person of the Year Award.

In 2005 he married a Japanese professional musician named Sayuri.

Interestingly the two things he has said that he was afraid of as a child and that can still cause him some anxiety today are the puppets and the scaled-down, single deck electric trolley bus (a.k.a. 'street car') that appeared in Mr Rogers' Neighbourhood, the American children's television series of the 1960s.

> *"Try to remember that being unsuccessful in school doesn't automatically mean that you'll be unsuccessful in life."*
> D. Pilkey

Daniel Handler

(a.k.a. Lemony Snicket)

- **Life span:** 28th February 1970 - present
- **Born:** San Francisco, California, U.S.A.
- **First book:** The Basic Eight (1998)

Before they retired from work Daniel's dad was an accountant (63) and his mum was a dean (64) in San Francisco's City College. He also had younger sister at home and they all enjoyed classical music. He even sang in the San Francisco Boys' Chorus in the 1980s.

As a young boy one of his fears was of being kidnapped by someone who might leap into his attic bedroom from the top of a tree that grew outside his window. However, as with the many successful play battles against evil that he and his Star Wars figures survived he was able to keep this particular fear under control.

At first he attended the Commodore Sloat Elementary School in San Francisco and then the Herbert Hoover Middle School soon becoming an enthusiastic reader. In particular he was fascinated by The Bears' Famous Invasion of Sicily by Dino Buzzati (1945), The Gashlycrumb Tinies (1963) by Edward Gorey and The Egypt Game (1967) by Zilpha Keatley Snyder. He also loved books by William K. Maxwell Jr. and Roald Dahl.

When he graduated from San Francisco's Lowell High School in 1988 he travelled over 4800 kms (3000 miles) to the other side of the country to the Wesleyan University in Connecticut to study for a B.A. degree (38) in English and American Studies before graduating in 1992.

By this time he was 22 he had begun to write poetry and although he won The Academy of American Poets Poets' Prize in 1990 and the Connecticut Student Poets' Prize in 1992 he was more interested in writing fiction.

Because his girlfriend hadn't yet finished her course at the same university that he was attending and as the result of being able to obtain a grant (65) from his university he was able afford to carry on living in the same city and to continue his creative writing efforts. It was there that he completed his first novel. However, because he wasn't satisfied with it he didn't make any effort to get it published.

In 1992 he returned to San Francisco where he worked as a part-time administrative assistant and part-time comedy writer for a radio show whilst working on his second novel.

Once his book "The Basic Eight" was almost finished he and his girlfriend decided to move to New York where he planned to work as a freelance (49) book critic and a film reviewer whilst trying to get his book published. However, his book was rejected several dozen times before it was finally published in 1998. This was followed by two further books in 2000 and 2006 written using his birth name.

His first two novels in the series "A Series of Unfortunate Events" about three orphaned children suffering numerous terrible events in a mock-Gothic parallel world were published between 1999-2006. These were followed by a second series between 2012-15. For this four-part series he used his pen-name Lemony Snicket and in these stories he explored Snicket's childhood and his apprenticeship in the Stain'd-by-the-Sea's Volunteer Fire Department.

He went on to write several other children's novels under the Snicket pen name, including two companion books linked to the series. Handler however, who has said that he dislikes 'syrupy sweet' stories (66), often warns his readers, tongue-in-cheek, (67) against reading or buying any of his Snicket books because they have unhappy beginnings, middles and endings.

Handler has made it clear that he doesn't believe that children need to be protected from unhappy events and instead, rather than avoiding things that are confusing, uncertain and unnerving, he invites his readers to tolerate feeling uncomfortable and to understand that life doesn't always happen in clear and easy-to-understand ways.

On the other hand however, his picture book: The Dark (2013) is one book he has been happy to recommend, especially to children who are afraid of the dark, because it includes helpful conversations between a little boy and 'The Dark' which take place in a dark basement.

Handler has enjoyed a lot of success amongst adults and children, impressing both groups with plays, films, and a Netflix series: A Series of Unfortunate Events (2017-19) including one episode in which Handler, a skilled accordion and keyboard player, plays the accordion music. Occasionally Handler also plays in a San Francisco based band The Magnetic Fields.

Although it has been calculated that his A Series of Unfortunate Events books have sold more than thirteen million copies, been translated into thirty-seven languages and been sold in over forty countries Handler has said - jokingly - that his books "have simply failed to fail" and therefore he has carried on writing them.

In 2012 his novel 'Why We Broke Up' (2011) won a 'Michael L. Printz Honor Award' and in 2017 he achieved a Peabody Award for excellence in Children's & Youth Programming. This was followed in 2019 by a Writers' Guild TV Award winner for a 2017 television play adaption of an episode from one of his A Series of Unfortunate Events books.

When talking about things that he hates about being a writer he has said that he hates "admitting that he's a writer; having other people tell him that they are writers; taking all day to write a single sentence; dropping pens; computers and the way they often break down, and finally, people telling him about things that they think would be good in one of his books but that are terrible ideas."

"If you are interested in stories with happy endings
you would be better off looking elsewhere."
D. Handler

Jeffrey Patrick Kinney

- **Life span:** 19 Feb 1971- present
- **Birthplace:** Fort Washington, Maryland, U.S.A.
- **First book:** The Diary of a Wimpy Kid (2007)

Brian Kinney, Jeff's dad, was an analyst in the Pentagon (68) and his mum Patricia graduated from university with a pre-schoolers' teaching qualification. Jeff grew up at home with an older brother and sister and a younger brother.

His first two schools were Potomac Landing Elementary School in Fort Washington and Eugene Burroughs Middle School in Accokeek, Maryland after which he attended the Bishop McNamara High School in Forestville, Fort Washington until 1989.

As a youngster Jeff enjoyed reading his dad's comic book collection that featured such Disney characters as Uncle Scrooge and Donald Duck. He also enjoyed reading his sister's Judy Blume books and books by Beverly Cleary, moving on later to books by J.R.R. Tolkien and the Anglo-American science fiction writer Piers Anthony.

It was a middle school teacher however, who helped him and some of his classmates to develop their jokes and their drawing skills with her constructive criticism. Later on, in high school, someone introduced him and a friend to Dungeons & Dragons, something that he has said helped him to hone his skills as a storyteller.

In 1989, when he was 18 years old, he was awarded a U.S. Air Force training scholarship and he began to study at Villanova University in Maryland. However, at the end of his first year he transferred to The University of Maryland to begin a four year course in computer science. It was whilst he was there, between 1990 and 1993, that he published his Igdoof cartoon strip for the university's newspaper. Then, in an attempt to create even more spare time for his cartoon work, he changed courses again, this time to a criminal law degree course; a move that was successful in this way.

At this stage in his life Kinney had already been working part-time as an online webpage designer with funbrain.com and it was on this company's website that he had begun uploading his stories about his Greg Heffley character; something that he did almost daily between 1992 – 2005.

He hoped that these achievements would help him move into a newspaper cartoon-drawing career but instead he received lots of rejection letters and because of this, and in order to earn a wage, he became obliged to accept newspaper layout work. He also took on work in software production and web design.

Although Jeff worked on his Heffley cartoons more extensively from 1998 onwards it was only after a further 8 years of effort that he felt ready to show his first book about his manipulative middle school weakling to a publisher.

The Diary of a Wimpy Kid was eventually published in 2007 after Kinney had agreed to adapt his online material into three books in the series that included Rodrick Rules in 2008 and The Last Straw in 2009. Other books that Kinney has written include The Wimpy Kid Do-It-Yourself Book (2008), The Wimpy Kid Movie Diary (2010), The Wimpy Kid Movie Diary: The Next Chapter (2017).

Big Shot (2021) in which Greg Heffley reluctantly sets out to see if he can achieve fame as a basketballer is Kinney's 16th book in The Diary of a Wimpy Kid series.

 Kinney has also published three books about Greg Heffley's best friend Rowley Jefferson: Diary of an Awesome Friendly Kid (2019), Rowley Jefferson's Awesome Friendly Adventures (2020), and Rowley Jefferson's Awesome Friendly Spooky Stories (2021), books that have also become bestsellers.

However, it is his Wimpy Kid books that have regularly skyrocketed to the No.1 position on various book sales charts, achieving worldwide sales of over 250 million copies in just 13 years and making this one of the top-five bestselling book series of all time. The Diary of a Wimpy Kid books have now been translated into 65 languages.

On March 19, 2010, his first of his Wimpy Kid films was released followed by Rodrick Rules in 2011, Dog Days in 2012, and The Long Haul in 2017.

Aside from the Wimpy Kid series, Jeff created Poptropica® an on-line adventure world where for kids could engage in quests, enjoy stories and play games as their own personally created.

Through this website children could travel to some of the games' many islands and enjoy story lines that were often rooted in factual history. They could also use gaming literacy to sharpen their problem-solving skills as well as solving mysteries that were unique to each island. Sadly though Jeff's increasing Wimpy Kids workload eventually led to him leave behind his involvement with Poptropica pre-2019.

Apart from achieving a Dorothy Canfield Fisher Children's Book Award in 2009, an award voted for by children Jeff has also received six Nickelodeon Kids'

Choice Awards for a number of his books. Moreover, his book successes have led him to staying at the top of the bookseller lists kept by the New York Times, the Wall Street Journal and Publisher's Weekly. In fact, his Wimpy Kid books are generally guaranteed to remain on the New York Times bestseller list for years after their publication – more than any other books – including those in the Harry Potter series.

In 2009 Kinney even appeared on Time magazine's list of the 100 Most Influential People in the World.

Jeff lives in Plainville, Southern Massachusetts, with his wife Julie whom he married in 2000 and their two sons. In May 2015, Kinney and his wife Julie opened a local bookstore and cafe in Plainville, Massachusetts called An Unlikely Story.

"It's our choices that make us who we are."
J. Kinney

In this final section Jeff Kinney shares some of his thoughts on his books and on his approach to writing them. So as you reach the end of this book I hope that you will enjoy this section as much as you have the rest of the book?

Bonus section

A few years ago during a discussion with an interviewer from Reading Rockets, a reading promotion charity, Jeff said this about his approach to writing:

> "I don't care all that much about the storyline in my books. I see my books as a way to deliver jokes. However, if I can also work out a way to get a good story out of the content then I'm very satisfied. My aim is to keep the reader laughing and often. If, however, I have too much of a plot it can get in the way of the jokes and the story burns through too many pages. So I often sacrifice a good story to introduce a good joke."

My books are like candy because they don't have a lot of intellectual growth vitamins in them. However, although kids do need their 'literature vitamins' any books that adults offer to kids shouldn't put them off reading. Adults need to meet kids at their current interest level, after which they may be able to introduce the child to some more sophisticated literature.

When I started writing it was for an adult audience. For 8 years or more I never even considered that I was writing for kids. I can't claim therefore that I was targeting reluctant readers or helping to get kids reading more, because I wasn't. However, if there is a lesson for me it is this, that if you try writing for kids there is a danger of dumbing down your writing. I aim to write what I'd like or maybe what my younger self might have liked after which I hope that my readers will find me in the text and appreciate what I've written.

I've always had a kid's sensibilities. I like things that kids like. I like the food that kids like. I feel as though everybody else grew up and that I missed getting the instructions for growing up when they were given out. Although I live in a very adult world, I'm really a kid at heart. I think that I'm in some sort of state of arrested development, although luckily I've been able to find a way to apply that to my work and it's working out well for me.

In his book "Outliers: The Story of Success" (2008) Malcolm Gladwell says that for anybody to be an expert at anything they need to spend about 10,000 hours developing their skills or knowledge. As a result when I started creating my Wimpy Kid books I spent about eight years, or to put it another way, close to 10,000 hours working and re-working my books and my characters. When I talk to kids, I tell them that when they have an idea they need to keep nurturing it and working on it. I remind them that although they might not be successful straight away, if they keep going they could end up with something really good. That's how I explain successful creativity.

Once I got the idea for The Diary of a Wimpy Kid I needed to nurture it. I wasn't in any sort of rush. I thought "Well if it takes a year that'll be okay, and if it takes ten years, which is about what it did take, that will be okay too." So I worked and worked on it in private until I was ready to show it to a publisher.

After that it was still hard because no-one wanted to see anything from someone like me who was unknown. However, I was lucky or maybe it was fate because I met an editor who had just published a web comic and because I started my comic on the web he was interested and he said "This is exactly what we're looking for." He responded to it emotionally and visually before even reading it. It was as though he saw it through a kid's eyes. As a university student my drawing skills weren't as good as those of a professional cartoonist, and when I tried to use them my creative writing in world of grown-ups I hit a wall. So I said to myself "Well, if my drawing abilities are simply like those of a 12 or 13 year-old, I'm going to act as though I'm drawing like that on purpose. So that's where the images for Greg Heffley came from."

In talking about how he actually writes his books Jeff has said this:

"Nowadays it takes me about nine months to create a book. I know that to create a good book I need between 350-400 images to start with before I start reducing them in number. Then, later on I'll consider the quality of the material. I always start thinking of my book in terms of jokes. I think of as many jokes as I can even if they are not linked. Then, later, hopefully there will enough jokes that relate to one another to enable me to develop a theme. So very often I don't know what the storyline is until a short time before my first draft is due to be handed in. I put my 350-400 ideas into a computer document and I award them values—points for each joke. So one joke might require a series of four images to reveal the joke, while another one might be a single-image joke. And then I'll count how many I have and then start arranging them in terms of themes. Then I'll outline my story in an extremely broad way perhaps using just three bullet points and then I'll expand and expand the material until I have enough material to write my first draft. Then after I've finished with my first draft, I'll start drawing toward the end of the project.

I can easily complete seven or eight versions of the book, improving the material as I go. It's hard work because humour is such a subjective thing and so I ask other people about which parts of the material they think are good and which are not so funny. I often test my first draft on half a dozen different sorts of people because individuals respond to things in different ways and I try to notice where there is agreement. I don't start on the drawing until I'm happy with the written material, because each of the drawings – approximately 350 per book – take me an hour. Obviously the final version of the book is much more polished and often it can be very different from the first draft."

Jeff Kinney

Glossary

(1)   Homemaker – the adult or older sibling assuming most of the responsibility for creating a home, caring for it and for those living in it, e.g. children

(2)   Jumping ship – refers to a sailor leaving his or her ship suddenly and unexpectedly without permission. It can also be used in describing the behaviour of someone who quits an organisation or place in a similar way.

(3)   Mutinied – committing mutiny involves openly rebelling against ones leaders

(4)   Beach bum – someone who spends a lot of time relaxing in a non work-related setting without obviously achieving very much.

(5)   Albino – unlike dark grey sperm whales, white sperm whales lack the melanin responsible for ensuring their normal colouring.

(6)   Customs Officer- someone paid to enforce the laws relating to individuals or items that are brought into a country or leave it.

(7)   Philosopher – someone who spends a lot of time considering the possible meanings of life.

(8)   The Fruitlands Commune – An experimental 19th century community in Harvard, USA that involved a group of unrelated friends and their children living and working together on a farm. An important part of their experiment involved spending time and effort considering the meaning of life.

(9)   The Women's Educational and Industrial Union – a group whose members held meetings that aimed to improve working conditions for women and children in three U.S. cities.

(10) A stroke – is when the blood either cannot reach a part of the brain due to a blockage or when the person has a bleed inside their head that presses on a part of their brain. Either of these can stop the brain working properly unless treated.

(11) A typesetter – a person who arranges physical or digital letters in the correct order so that letters and words can either be inked and printed onto a page or produced digitally as text.

(12)   "Mark twain" (Literally "mark number two") – a phrase that was called out loudly by a sailor at the front of a steamboat to confirm that there was enough water beneath it. By reporting how far the level of

water rose up towards a mark on a measuring rope the sailor would be informing the person steering the boat whether the water was two fathoms deep, i.e. at least 12 feet (3.7m) and that it was safe for the boat to continue.

(13) Satire – a style of humorous writing, acting or behaviour in which a person shines a spotlight on behaviour, attitudes, rules, social class that he or she finds unacceptable with the aim of correcting them.

(14) An impresario – a person whose career involves organising and staging concerts, plays, operas, ballet and dance performances. He or she may also pay to stage these events.

(15) The Great Plains – before these became used for agriculture the plains were vast stretches of flat grassland or scrubland. They were affected by bitterly cold winters and extremely hot and humid summers. At first there were no roads across them and few people could afford to travel on the developing railway services.

(16) Dug-outs (a.k.a. pit houses) – these were deep 'family size' hollows in the ground with canvas or log coverings at ground level or above to protect the inhabitants.

(17) Diphtheria – this, plus smallpox and measles, were common infectious diseases in the 1800s and 1900s.

(18) A stock market crash – this is when adults who have put some of their spare cash into owning parts of commercial companies realise that their 'documents of ownership' have suddenly become much less valuable. When this happens, and too many people try to get their money refunded at the same time, the system for selling their ownership certificates and getting their money back often crashes.

(19) A drug store – a shop that includes a pharmacy section. It may also sell toiletries, cosmetics, household and other products.

(20) Tuberculosis (a.k.a. T.B.) – a disease that can affect the lungs and the bones. Humans can get it by drinking infected milk that has not been heat-treated to kill germs. The B.C.G vaccination can be given to people who live in "high T.B. risk" areas to help protect them.

(21) Baptist Church Minister – after the English king Henry VIII created the Church of England in 1534 some Christians believed that the new churches were still too much like the original Roman Catholic Church and so instead of staying part of the Church of England they developed independent Baptist groups with their own priests or vicars called ministers or pastors.

(22) A proof reader – someone who looks for spelling, grammar, punctuation and formatting errors in text.

(23) Honeymoon – a holiday that newly married couples sometimes take after their wedding. The word is linked to an old European custom of giving newlyweds enough mead (a.k.a. honey wine) to last them one month.

(24) Royalties – a share of the profits that are owed to a writer, a screenwriter or scriptwriter as a result of the success of a story, book, play or film.

(25) Jute mill – a factory where the fibres from a tall plant similar to bamboo are spun into yarn for making rope, matting and sacking.

(26) Vagrant – a homeless person thought to be capable of working but who is not doing so and who lives through begging or minor crime. They may move around a town or city or move from city to city. Vagrancy laws were largely abolished in the USA in 1983.

(27) Degradation – situations, conditions or experiences considered by most people to be shameful or disgusting.

(28) Cramming School (a.k.a. 'a crammer') – an academy in which pupils are helped to cram in (squeeze in) large amounts of information into their brains in a short amount of time to help them pass a test or exam.

(29) Socialism – one way that society can be organised. Socialists believe that everyone, but workers in particular, should be treated well and fairly and they try to consider the fairest ways to create wealth and how to spread it evenly.

(30) Disembarking – leaving a ship or an aircraft.

(31) Gold panning – swirling a small amount of river water around in a shallow dish to separate out any small pieces of gold from the sand and gravel that remain once the water is swished out.

(32) Diplomats – **officials** whose **job** it is to **represent** one **country** in other countries. They usually **work** in **embassy** offices.

(33) A cat with nine lives – a description given to someone who survives multiple dangerous situations without being permanently harmed.

(34) Copywriter – following a great deal of preparation a copywriter writes attention grabbing text for publicity material.

(35) Animator – someone who often works with small, large or even huge models in such a way as to make them appear to be alive. A cartoonist

however, is someone who creates static images and cartoon strips that can later be made to appear to move.

(36)   Maiden name – an unmarried women's birth surname which she can legally change if she wishes to when she gets married.

(37)   Prohibition laws – laws that made it illegal to produce and sell alcohol. These were introduced when authorities became worried that adults were drinking too much alcohol.

(38)   B.A. degree – a Bachelor of Arts degree. The title of the qualification awarded to a university student when he or she has been successful in their exams after several years of study. This qualification relates to the subject they have studied and not necessarily to the creation of any art. Neither does the student have to be a bachelor (an unmarried person) to study for a B.A degree.

(39)   Master's degree – a university qualification awarded to a student who has studied their chosen subject at a very high level, i.e. who has shown mastery of their subject and who has met the university's examination requirements.

(40)   The Great Depression – a widespread collapse of banks and businesses between 1929-40 when American companies, banks and citizens were not making the large profits that they had previously made. Many companies, factories and farms failed and millions of people lost their jobs and their homes.

(41)   Japanese Americans – Americans with full or partial Japanese backgrounds. In the 1950s there were more than 25,000 Japanese-Americans living in the USA, mainly in California.

(42)   Seamstress – someone who earns a wage from sewing and mending.

(43)   Elope – this is when two young lovers leave home secretly to get married without the permission of their parents or guardians.

(44)   Reality writer – someone who describes things as they are rather than over using his or her imagination.

(45)   Memoir – a piece of writing about part of someone's life or an experience of theirs.

(46)   Honorary – a title or qualification given to an individual as an honour to show respect to them without them having had to study for that qualification.

(48)   Propaganda – information designed to make people feel a certain way or to believe certain things.

(49) Freelance – this is when someone choses to work on short projects that they are paid for upon completion instead of working for an employer permanently.

(50) Commission – an order or instruction to a person or a group to create and complete a piece of work or a product.

(51) Typography – the arrangement of words, letters, numbers and symbols ready for reproduction as text or digitally.

(52) Graphic design – the production of images and appealing written language for display purposes.

(53) Conscripted – when an individual is compelled by law to serve in a country's military services.

(54) Collage – a work of art created by pasting various materials that are not normally associated with each another onto a surface.

(55) Anthropology – the study of human beings from prehistoric times to today and the ways these groups live (or previously lived), i.e. their cultures.

(56) Off the cuff – without any preparation, spontaneously.

(57) Stillborn – an unborn baby that dies while still inside the mother or who dies whilst being born. "Still" i.e. with no evidence of life.

(58) People who have a bi-polar illness can occasionally experience much stronger emotions than most other people do. During such periods they may become wildly excited or seriously sad for varying lengths of time in a see-saw pattern.

(59) Stereotype – an idea or belief that lots of people seem to have about an object or group based upon either how it seems or looks. The idea or belief that the individuals or the group have about the other people or the object may be untrue or only partly true.

(60) Anthology – a collection of short stories or poems by different authors assembled into a single volume for publication as one book.

(61) Chaplain – a person with helps people to meet their religious needs but who works somewhere other than in a church, e.g. in a hospital, prison, a school, a university or a military unit.

(62) ADHD – an individual with ADHD may have an overactive brain and experience difficulties in keeping still, paying attention and in making the best behavioural choices.

(63) Accountant – someone who keeps or examines the records of money received, paid and owed by a company, or a group, or an individual in order to help them make decisions about how to use and save money.

(64) Dean – In a university the dean is the head of a number of departments with responsibilities for hiring staff, planning, financial matters and administrative duties as well as for some educational input.

(65) A grant – an award of money for one's day-to-day expenses and other necessities e.g. accommodation.

(66) Syrupy sweet – likeable but artificial and unrealistic.

(67) Tongue in cheek – where something is intended to be understood as a joke even though the speaker seems to appear to be serious.

(68) The Pentagon – the headquarters (i.e. offices mainly) of the U.S. Department of Defence, Arlington, Virginia built in 1946.

Resources

I would specifically like to acknowledge the usefulness of the following in the preparation of some of the profiles:

Generic sources

https://americanliterature.com/authors

https://www.worldcat.org (book or other format search)

https://www.worldcat.org/identities (i.e. author search)

Louisa May Alcott

The Spirit of America bookstore website

L. Frank Baum

International Wizard of Oz Club, https://ozclub.org/oz-timeline/1842-1899-l-frank-baums-early-career/

Daniel Handler (a.k.a. Lemony Snicket)

Encyclopedia of World Biography website - https://www.notablebiographies.com/news/Sh-Z/Snicket-Lemony-Daniel-Handler.html

Laura Ingalls-Wilder

https://www.famousauthors.org/laura-ingalls-wilder

Jack London

Jack London International website – www.jack-london.org

The Art of Manliness website - The Life of Jack London as a Case Study in the Power and Perils of Thumos. Episode 1 https://www.artofmanliness.com/articles/the-life-of-jack-london-as-a-case-study-in-thumos-1-introduction/

Herman Melville

The Life and Works of Herman Melville – www.melville.org –

L. M. Montgomery

The L.M. Montgomery Institute - https://lmmontgomery.ca/about/lmm/her-life

The Abandoned Carousel website - L.M. Montgomery/Canadian World/Anne of Green Gables: A History, Episode 30 https://theabandonedcarousel.com/lucy-maud-montgomery-canadian-world-anne-of-green-gables/

Richard M. Scarry

www.richardscarry.com

Maurice Sendak

Tufts University webpage (tufts-mmm.tufts.edu) https://mma.pages.tufts.edu/fah188/sendak/bio.html

Photo credits

All author photos are in the Public Domain on Wikipedia, except those listed below.

Eric Carle	By Fred Rockwood - https://www.flickr.com/photos/freeloosedirt/3474521853/, CC BY-SA 2.0, https://commons.wikimedia.org/w/index.php?curid=106007954
Daniel Handler	By permission of the author
Jeffrey Kinney	By Filip Wolak Photography, NYC
Madeleine L'Engle Camp	By permission of Charlotte Jones Voiklis Credit Judith Petrovich
Lucy Maud Montgomery	Credit Library and Archives Canada / C-011299
Robert Munsch	By permission of the author
David Murray Pilkey	By Kojisasuke - Own work, CC BY-SA 4.0, https://commons.wikimedia.org/w/index.php?curid=81284072
Richard Scarry	By permission of Huck Scarry
E. B. White	By White Literary LLC, CC BY-SA 3.0, https://commons.wikimedia.org/w/index.php?curid=14518529